DISCOVERING
Lascaux

© Editions SudOuest, 2006.
Photogravure by Labogravure à Bordeaux (33).
This book was printed by Pollina in Luçon (85) - n° L54133
ISBN: 978-2-87901-706-8
Editeur: 20204.04.06.06.10

DISCOVERING
Lascaux

Brigitte and Gilles Delluc

Photographs by Ray Delvert
Translated by Angela Caldwell

ÉDITIONS SUD OUEST

Bulls' Chamber

The "unicorn" (length approx. 2.40 m) thickly outlined in black.
A composite animal (the body of a rhinoceros, the withers of a bear or bison,
the head and spots of a big cat and the tail of a horse), or an imaginary
drawing of a feline as described in the oral tradition. The two "horns"
might be the lines of the tail of the first large bull. Two horses lightly drawn
in red on the body. To the right is a brown horse (the head was rubbed away
by a falling splinter of rock). This enigmatic "unicorn" is the first large
drawing you see as you enter the cave.

Bulls' Chamber

The second large bull (length approx. 3.50 m) depicted with genitals and a thick neck. The animal is characteristic of the style used to represent cattle in Lascaux i.e. the head seen in profile and the horns from three-quarter view, the ear protruding from the nape of the neck, the enormous body seen in profile with the breast seen from three-quarter view, short legs in motion, and hooves seen from the front (massive ovals separated into two cloots, or sections) with a spur above them. The shoulder has a barbed marking. A small red stag overlays the back legs and a red bison overlays the line of the belly.

Bulls' Chamber
A group of stags between the first two bulls (each stag is approx.
70 cm in length). They have slender heads, a complex set of antlers
and legs thrown stiffly out to the front and back in a rigid gallop.

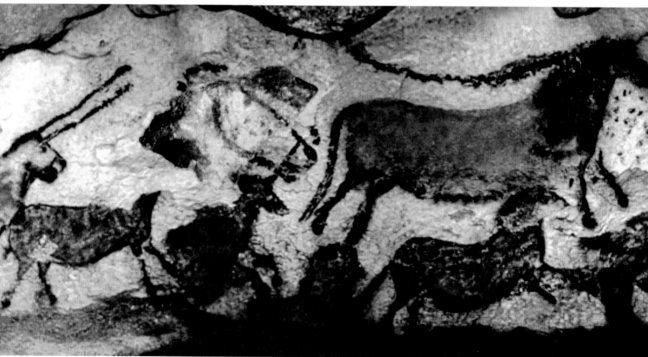

Opposite:

Bulls' Chamber

The lower clay sections of the rock walls are irregular. The huge paintings decorate the edge of the roof, covered with crystallised white calcite. At the end of the chamber is the entrance to the narrow Axial Gallery; to the right, is the entrance to the Passage (Glory collection, MNHN).

Bulls' Chamber

Between the "unicorn" and the first bull, a large flake of rock has come away from the wall, taking part of the painting with it. What remains is the muzzle of an animal outlined in black, like the nearby bulls. Thanks to a photograph of the flake of rock, taken shortly after the chamber was discovered, it was possible to reconstitute the painting in its original state, showing the head of a large horse (reconstitution by Delluc based on two photographs by Glory).

Bulls' Chamber

A few days after discovering the cave, Marcel Ravidat posed in front of the paintings of the great bulls to add an idea of scale (Laval collection).

The entrance to the cave today lies in the woods at Lascaux

Of course, the opening has been widened and deepened but, from a distance in 1940, the original entrance and surrounding countryside looked like this (photograph by Delluc).

Un pays

Bulls' Chamber. The first large bull, or auroch (length approx. 3 m), outlined with a thick black line. The horns and withers are highlighted in red. Beside the bull is a row of small brown horses and a large red horse with a black head.

The Vézère Valley,
The dawn of the Magdalenian Period,
The reindeer and a few other creatures
The Cro-Magnons

The cave at Lascaux is an extraordinary
coming-together of a country, a moment
in time, animals and men.

And this is no doubt what makes
this decorated cave unique.

A country

The Vézère flowing between hills and cliffs

At this point along its course, the black river, still full of marl and mica from the borders of Corrèze and pebbles from the Limousin, flows through a wide valley flanked by fields of tobacco and maize, or fields of poplar trees and meadows, at the foot of the gently-rolling limestone hills of "Dark Périgord". It is here that Man built Montignac, a traditional small country town overlooked by a castle.

In Corrèze, further upstream, the Vézère flows for miles through the narrow gorges of crystalline Limousin rocks. Downstream, beyond Thonac, it gouges out a difficult, grandiose passage through the limestone of Le Moustier, La Madeleine and Les Eyzies between cliffs riddled with caves and rock shelters. This river is both a major route in and out of the area and part of its lifeblood. On its banks, human settlements have existed for the past 400,000 years.

Its tributaries are modest waterways, no more than a few streams, most of them dry cwms slicing into the plateau, dividing it into a myriad of small uplands, hills or mounds, some bare, others covered with a few trees. One such is the hill at Lascaux, on the left bank of the Vézère. In Dark Périgord, limestone predominates, forming cliffs, rocks, tall cliffs, gritty slopes and uplands hidden in some places beneath a thin covering of earth or sand. This is Coniacian, a yellow rock rich in iron, which reddens when exposed to heat. It is coarse-grained, and as full of sand particles as it is of limestone. It is broken up by a small number of faults but most often it is cracked by diaclases that open the way for the underground streams which gouge out the countless caverns.

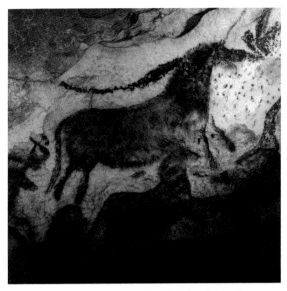

Bulls' Chamber. A red horse with a black head (length approx. 2m). The ears are perked up and the head is small in comparison with the remainder of the body. The short legs are thrown forwards and backwards in a contrived "canter". The front left leg is detached from the chest by a twist of perspective.

One cave among thousands

Périgord is the land of the thousand caves. From the water sinks through which they seep, the rivers make their way underground, vigorously drilling a passage for themselves at the expense of the vertical fractures or the joints separating the horizontal strata in the rock. In some places, the ceiling of the subterranean galleries has collapsed, forming a modest pothole, or "aven". Often these networks of underground passages were subjected to later invasion by red clay, sand or stalagmites. On the hillsides, some of the entrances have been blocked up. Often, the streams have abandoned the galleries, to run deeper and deeper down in the earth.

And so there are the dry, fossilised caves that we can visit today, narrow tunnels with barely enough space for potholers to squeeze through or beautiful spacious caverns, some of which have been laid out to cater for visitors.

Some of the larger caves (approximately thirty of them, plus a dozen rock shelters) were decorated by prehistoric man from the Aurignacian c. 35,000 years ago until the

Bulls' Chamber. The face to face of the first two bulls.

Between their horns, a red horse and a group of small red stags.

MARCEL RAVIDAT, DISCOVERER OF LASCAUX

The apprentice mechanic was 18 years old. On 8th September 1940, alerted by Robot, his dog with a long russet-coloured coat, he discovered the entrance to the cave – a mere hole in the ground. The young man was obstinate and adventurous. He wanted to get into the tunnel but it would need to be widened. On 12th September, armed with a knife and torches, he forced his way through the narrow entrance and slid down the sloping floor of the cave. He was dazzled by what he and his three friends (Georges Agniel, Simon Coencas and Jacques Marsal) saw. The lads told the schoolteacher, Léon Laval, about their discovery and he became the cave's first curator. Father Henri Breuil, the "Pope of Prehistory", arrived a short time later. With Jacques Marsal, who came from Montignac like him, Ravidat acted as keeper of the cave which was soon overrun by visitors. A short time later, he became a member of the French Resistance. He went on to fight in Germany. What was his reward? As soon as the cave was opened to the public in 1948, he became one of its guides, with Jacques Marsal, and he remained so until the cave was finally closed in 1963. It was Marcel Ravidat who detected the first signs of the "green disease" in 1957-1958.

Discoverer Marcel Ravidat. Standing guard near his tent, he keeps watch over his discovery during the autumn of 1940 (Laval collection).

end of the Magdalenian some 10,000 years ago. The smallest is only a few yards long; the largest, spreading over several miles, is now equipped with a small underground railway. It is a well-known fact that many of the cave mouths and shelters provided a ready-made awning for the homes, or even the tombs, of Neanderthal or Cro-Magnon Man. Yet no prehistoric settlement has been discovered here far below the surface. Cave men did not actually live in caves. At least not in Périgord.

Faced with a choice of a thousand caverns, Cro-Magnon Man selected the one on the hill in Lascaux 17,000 years ago as the setting for the most outstanding underground sanctuary in prehistory. This is one of the largest caves in the area and its walls were the most suitable for painting, engraving and mural art.

There was little merit in Man's having discovered this cave. At that time, its porch, the outlet of an age-old subterranean stream dating from the early Tertiary Era, lay wide open at the foot of a sheer cliff, amidst a few stunted oaks, pines, hazelnut bushes and junipers on a sun-drenched, arid plateau.

Advancing into the cave along this fossilised waterway, tallow lamps lit up a vast rotunda (the **Bulls' Chamber**) and a narrow diaclase (the **Axial Gallery**). Grafted onto the side of it beyond a low gallery that can only be visited on hands and knees (the **Passageway**) was the lofty diaclase known as the **Nave**, with its two extensions. To the right is the wider **Apse** containing the **Pit** while at the end is the narrow corridor known as **The Felines' Gallery**. It is a complex layout spread over 250 metres but limited to two main galleries – one forming the entrance (Bulls' Chamber, Axial Gallery) and the other, deeper one consisting of the Passageway and Felines' Gallery. The first of these galleries is easy to visit; the second is steeper, with low roofs on some sections and two small shafts.

First and foremost, though, it was an empty cave. A layer of waterproof marl gave it an impenetrable roof through which the chalky water was unlikely to seep, trickle or

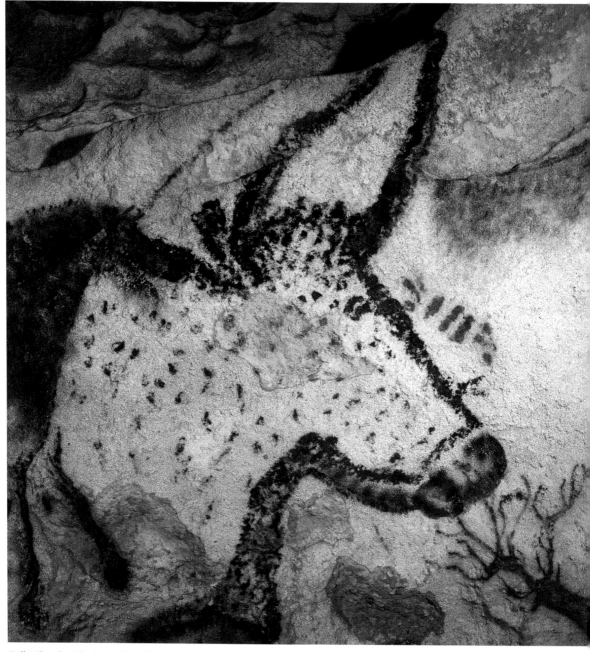

Bulls' Chamber. The head of the first large bull. The horns are set on the top of the head, to each side of the striped tuft of hair. The eye is depicted by means of two lines. The white muzzle is separated from the cheek by a curved line.

The head and neck are dotted with black spots. There is a symbol in front of the head consisting of short red lines.

Bulls' Chamber. The head of the second large bull, which faces the first one. The horns are shown from three-quarter view (one is C-shaped and the other forms an "S"), which is a typical way of portraying perspective in Lascaux.

The ear is set on the nape of the neck. The tuft of hair on the head is depicted by two parallel lines. There are dots around the eye. Between the two bulls is a red horse, with no legs. It has a brown body, the mane is fluffy and its ears are perked up.

Bulls' Chamber. A brown stag heavily outlined in black. The two antlers (with double tines) point forwards from the top of the head, a traditional feature of the deer in Lascaux, with one branch pointing vertically upwards and the other slanting backwards.
Behind the antlers is a short line that marks the ear. The abdomen has a paler strip. There is no tail. The hooves are oval and elongated with a pointed tip. Above them is a spur. The hooves are cloven, with each section separated by a membrane.
They are depicted as if seen from below.

André Glory. On the left, the young potholer with all the equipment for his favourite pasttime. On the right, an idealised picture of the same person standing in front of one of the cave walls in Lascaux, on the cover of one of his books.

FATHER GLORY AND HIS LIFEBELT

Father André Glory (1906-1966) is "the Lascaux Man". He was the only person to have studied the wall paintings and ground, work requiring painstaking patience. He was born in Alsace and was a potholer before becoming an expert in prehistory. He gave more than ten years of his life to the cave, working almost totally without payment before, eventually, becoming an engineer with the national research agency, the CNRS. He died in a road traffic accident, without having published his work.

In his youth, the brave tenacious researcher had his portrait done, dressed as a potholer-explorer. He wore a mechanic's overalls, stout boots and a helmet, and carried a carbide lamp and haversacks. He also carried a rope ladder and, round his waist, wore the inner tube from a car tyre as a lifebelt.

Some time later, to decorate the cover of one of Father Glory's works, an illustrator wanted to use a potholer admiring the Stag Frieze in Lascaux. He used the over-equipped explorer as a model for his work. The artist sketched him, still wearing his lifebelt, in a cave in which there is not the smallest trickle of water.

run. This cave has none of the stalactites, stalagmites or flowstones (calcite flows) that usually adorn the walls of Périgord's caves. On the contrary, the un-damaged roof and walls, almost totally free of peeling or scaling, are simply covered (in the Bulls' Chamber and Axial Gallery) with an immaculate, even layer of calcite, which may have crystallised when the cavity was filled with water in days long gone. The lower sections of the walls are covered with a more clayey substance. In the other passageways, the rough yellow rock is nearly always bare. The ground consists of clay and sand through-out the

cave, although the first chamber contains gours, concretions that were formed by low dams across a temporary stream. The calcite-covered walls of the Bulls' Chamber and Axial Gallery entrance, sparkling with small, hard, white crystals, were only painted. The engravings and a number of paintings including certain engraved details decorate the walls of the other yellow ochre siliceous galleries in which the limestone altered gradually, as if changing one grain at a time.

There was, then, a twofold choice – the choice of this cave rather than any of the many others, and the choice

Bulls' Chamber. A red stag with a too lavish, disorderly set of antlers. The ear protrudes from the nape of the neck.

Bulls' Chamber. A stag (length approx. 70 cm) crossing the breast of the third large bull. The design and size are identical to that of the stag in photo p.18.

of the technique used for the graphics, which was selected to suit the existing state of the cave walls.

As far as the cave itself is concerned, we have learnt much that was totally unknown to the Magdalenians. The porch of their cave-sanctuary collapsed relatively soon after they left it, following successive periods of ice and thaw, closing off the entrance to the network of underground passages for 17,000 years. In this forgotten microcosm, an independent climate established itself, regulated by almost imperceptible draughts that slowly kept the damp air moving while the low temperature was maintained by a huge conical rock fall. This prevented any condensation on the walls and evacuated the carbon dioxide that was produced naturally.

The artefacts left behind by the painters, engravers and visitors in prehistoric times remained in place, on the ledges of the walls and on the ground where they gradually became buried by layers of grit that fell off the walls, consisting of a thin layer of clay, a thin stalagmite floor or even the thick calcite of the gours. This archaeological security system was doubly effective because it was sealed by a few inches of sediment in an enclosed cave. And these remains have enabled us to reconstitute the lifestyle of those who once occupied the cave.

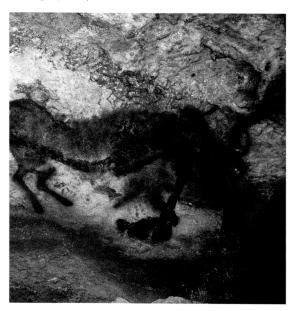

Bulls' Chamber. A red bison that blends into the line of the belly on the second large bull. The head and hump are massive; the front legs are merely sketched in, forming a V-shape. The horns are depicted in the usual way i.e. the one nearest from the observer is a C-shape while the furthest horn forms an "S".

Bulls' Chamber. The fourth large bull (length approx. 5.50 metres). The breast rises above the hind quarters of the third large bull, partly concealing it (giving an effect of perspective). The head, which has been damaged by a rock fall, has excessively large horns. To each side of the animal are signs and symbols – an oblique cross, a thick line and a row of dots, a rectilinear sign with a barb which seems to have been stabbed into the muzzle, and a small black line in front of the mouth (perhaps representing the animal's breath?). At its feet, in a position similar to that of the bison shown in page 20, is a red cow with horns outlined in black, followed by a small red animal that was not completed (it may have been a calf).

A country

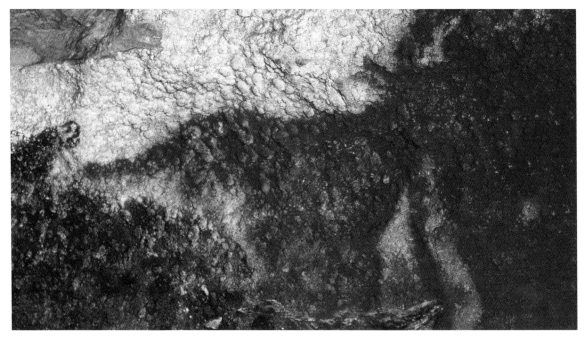

Bulls' Chamber. Between the bear and the red cow, also merging into the underbelly line of the third bull, is a small calf following its mother. This is one of the few paleolithic representations of a young animal.

Bulls' Chamber. A bear (length approx. 60 cm) painted in black. The outline blends almost completely into the line of the belly of the third large bull. The head is visible, with its two round ears, as are the narrow muzzle raised expectantly, the protruding withers, the rounded back and the end of one back paw with its claws.

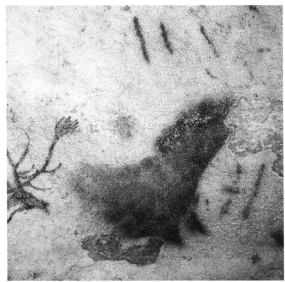

Bulls' Chamber. An unfinished painting of a small three-coloured horse on the shoulder of the third large bull (the head was destroyed by a rock fall). The mane consists of black stripes. Around the animal are numerous stick-shaped signs.

Almost everything to hand

The Magdalenian Period was neither a time of terror nor a golden age. Apart from rock shelters, the Vézère Valley provided the men of Lascaux with stone, timber and animals.

The pigments they required were in the ground – the yellow ochre and browns that reddened in the fire (a mixture of sand and clay, with iron oxide that was more or less dehydrated), the black manganese (or at least the manganese dioxide) and even charcoal. The limestone on the hillside could be split into small flakes which made excellent lamps, pallets and crushers for pigments. Flint was fairly common everywhere.

In those days, Périgord had no large forests. Saplings were cut from neighbouring trees to make climbing poles and scaffolding while the bushes provided the vegetable fibre used to make ropes.

There was animal life in abundance – large herbivores, big cats, small animals and birds. Yet it was the reindeer that was most important to Magdalenian man, providing him with food and various materials. This was, indeed, the Age of the Reindeer.

Bulls' Chamber. A spatter of stick-shaped signs beneath the belly of the fourth large bull. Large numbers of geometric signs such as these can be seen in Lascaux, either interlinked with each other or connected with the animals. Their meaning remains a mystery.

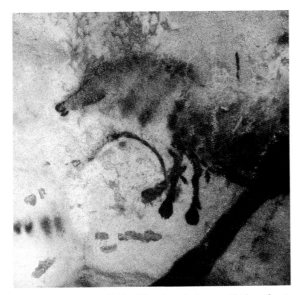

Bulls' Chamber. An unfinished drawing of a horse with three front legs. The animal seems to be emerging from the right front leg of the third large bull and be heading for the Axial Gallery.

Axial Gallery. After the vast Bulls' Chamber, the cave tapers to form a narrow gallery. The top of the walls and the roof are decorated with paintings.

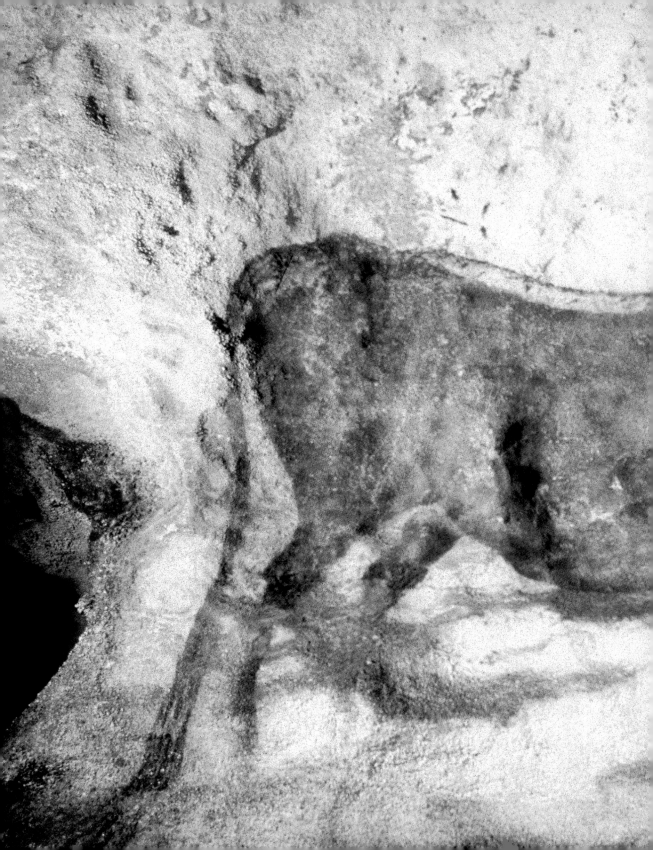

Axial Gallery

A red cow with a black head (length approx. 2.80 m).
The head and neck are slender, the horns are shown
in normal perspective, the body is enormous,
the frail legs are in marked perspective and the tail
is disproportionately long. The coat is dappled.
A paler stroke follows the line of the back (indicating
the coat or merely a second outline?). The cow is drawn
at the entrance to the gallery opposite the large stag
(cf. photo p. 29). Here, as elsewhere in Lascaux,
the lower section of the rock face, which is rough
and dirty, has not been decorated.

Axial Gallery

The two most famous "Chinese horses"
(in fact there are six in all, three on each wall of rock,
facing each other). They are typical of the artistic
precepts evident in all the paintings in Lascaux
i.e. they have a small slender head, an enormous
belly with indications of the coats, two shoulder
stripes, short legs shown in movement,
and rounded hooves seen from front view.
Given the raised front legs on the horse on the left,
the photo may well represent a stallion following a mare.

Axial Gallery. A red cow (length approx. 2.40 m). The front legs are raised while the hind legs merge into the first of the "Chinese horses" (head and neck emphasised by large black dots). In place of the horse's front legs, there is a symbol in the shape of a bracket, again consisting of dots. There are numerous signs all around this painting (dots, sticks, crosses branches).

Axial Gallery. An unfinished painting of a stag with a slender head and pointed ear (height 1.35 m). The stag has a mass of antlers with double tines and bays and wide palms bearing the curved tips. Below is a rectangular sign and a row of dots. The stag is flanked by three horses.

One moment in time

With a few grains of pollen

Flowers die, leaves and wood root; but pollen, like all plant spores, resists the passage of time. A durable husk ensures that these microscopic particles, of a shape and size characteristic of each individual species of plant, remain indestructible. For palynologists, they describe the plant environment and, by extension, the climate that was prevalent when the archaeological layer from which they are extracted was first laid down. Examination under a microscope of splinters of wood which have survived to the present day (this is highly unusual) provide similar information. The appearance of the sediments of each layer on a prehistoric site will also depend on the climate and on conditions when the deposits were laid down.

Cro-Magnon Man (like his immediate predecessors, Neanderthal Man or Le Moustier Man) was subjected to climatic cooling, better known as Wurm glaciation (from 75,000 B.C. to 10,000 B.C.). Yet Europe did not become one vast glacial wasteland. In our countries, although the weather was cooler with annual mean temperatures 5°C lower than today, Man was nevertheless able to live a normal life. Moreover, the climate varied depending on the era, the latitude, the altitude and distance from

the sea. Such variations had marked consequences on the flora and fauna.

During the period in which Lascaux was inhabited, the climate underwent a fairly humid rise in temperatures which lasted for somewhat less than one thousand years and was preceded and followed by colder periods. This intermediate stage in Lascaux was not uncommon and was, itself, subdivided into various warmer or colder periods. In fact, because Lascaux was situated in Périgord, in a geographical location that is equidistant from the Pole and the Equator, and from the sea and the mountains, the inhabitants enjoyed a climate very similar to our own i.e. approximately 10°C in January and a range of 15° to 22°C in July. Rainfall varied from 500 to 700 mm per year. The winters were fairly long but temperate, the summers were short and not very hot, and the springs and autumns were brief. As for the scenery around the hill at Lascaux, it was not very different (except for the housing and crops) to the landscape before us today.

The palynologist, Arlette Leroi-Gourhan, saw the landscape take shape under her microscope. The Magdale-

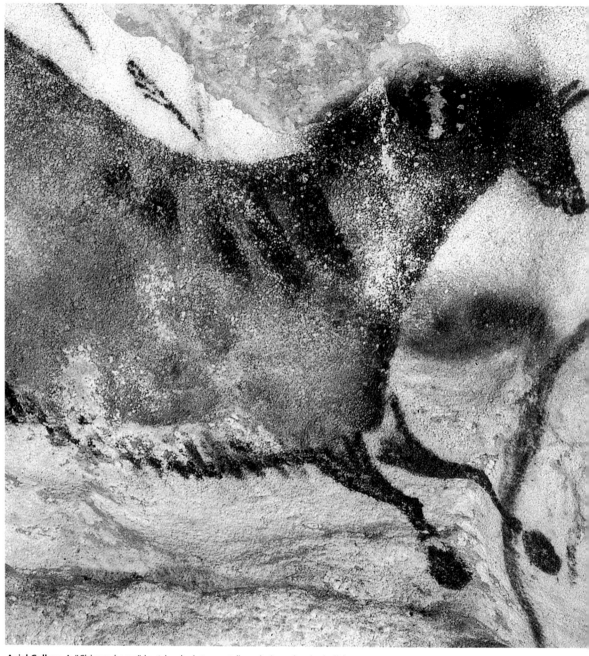

Axial Gallery. A "Chinese horse" in striped winter coat (long hair under the belly).
A break in the painting on the front and back left legs adds perspective and emphasises the foreground.

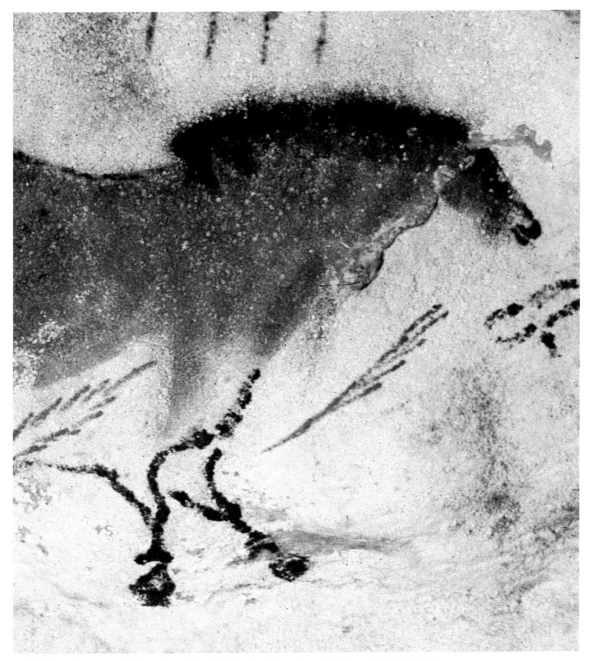

Axial Gallery. The yellow "Chinese horse" (length 1.40 m) with a pale coat (the breast is highlighted
by natural roughness in the rock). The light M-shaped markings on the belly are common in graphics of the Magdalenian Period.

ANDRÉ MALRAUX

The author of Antimémoires described a hidden cache of weapons in Lascaux in 1944 in a very heroic style: "Red and blue parachutes were spread out on the ground. On them were boxes and boxes. Like two animals from a future time, two machine guns stood on their tripods like Egyptian cats on their front legs, keeping watch over the store. On the roof covered with a sort of saltpetre ran magnificent dark animals, carried away in the movement of the round beams of our torches like emblems in flight. The shadows of bison hunters were probably once the shadows of giants when projected by the flames of resin torches…" (Malraux, 1972)

This admirable text was a dream and not a reality. In 1944, everybody knew about the cave; it could not be used as a hiding place. A German prehistorian had even been sent there for a short time.

André Malraux did not visit Lascaux until 1967 but it was under his authority, as Minister of Cultural Affairs, that the cave was finally closed in April 1963 and work began on its conservation.

André Malraux. The author of the "Imaginary Museum" visited the cave on 12th March 1967. The curator, Max Sarradet (right), accompanied him during the visit (photo by Jacques Lagrange, Pilote 24).

nians arrived in the cave during a period of climatic warming and left it as soon as they began to feel the effects of the cold era which followed it. This means that the first inhabitants lived in thick forest with hazelnut bushes, pines and tall broad-leaved trees such as oak, lime, elm, ash, hornbeam and sycamore. Below this cover grew privet, currant bushes, black alders and clematis. Here and there, there were even a few trees that demanded a warmer climate (e.g. maritime pines and walnut trees). When the climate became less attractive, the great deciduous trees became more sparse and the countryside was covered in a vegetation that was part tundra (there were Compositae such as centaury and thistles then Graminaceae, or grasses).

The fauna was such as might be expected in a temperate climate i.e. horses and cattle, deer, ibex, wild boar, brown bears, hares and rabbits, dormice, hedgehogs, frogs and bats. Yet a few species accustomed to colder climes also existed, among them the woolly rhinoceros and, perhaps, the musk ox. Most of all, though, there were the reindeer which spent the summer months on the slopes of the Massif Central.

A handful of charcoal

The plant world does not only provide prehistorians with pollen. When charcoal has been preserved, as it was in Lascaux, it can be carbon-dated.

Living organisms, whether animal or vegetable, contain the same proportion of natural carbon (carbon 12) and radioactive carbon (carbon 14) as the atmosphere. When exchanges cease after death, carbon 14 gradually diminishes, in line with a known decrease in radioactivity. Nowadays, measurement of the remaining carbon 14 can be used to determine the exact moment of death.

The charcoal preserved in the one and only archaeological layer of the soil in Lascaux was collected and examined using this method. On average, it is 17,000 years old (to be precise, 17,070 give or take 130 years).

And the objects found in this same layer (flint flakes and spearheads) are of the type used by Man at that time (Early Magdalenian).

Axial Gallery. A view of the end of the gallery, looking towards the Bulls' Chamber. On the right is the great black bull, a horse and a sign.

Axial Gallery

The reddish horse (length 3 m) outlined in black seems to be moving away towards the end of the gallery. The mane and beard are feathery and the breast and neck are clearly stencilled in. The hindquarters and hind legs are somewhat clumsy. Again there is a branch-shaped symbol in front of the animal. Below is a rocky traverse that was used to wedge the joists of the scaffolding on which the Magdalenian painters worked.

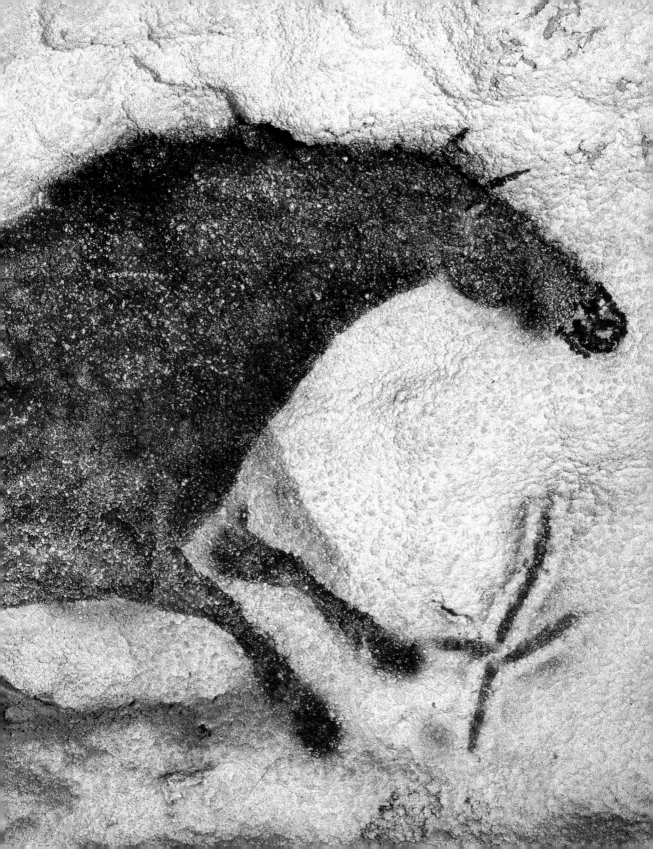

Axial Gallery

The "leaping" cow (length 1.70 m) facing the great black bull, a picture that is unusually full of movement. The hind legs are raised in a position that is anatomically incorrect and the tail is curved like a whip. In front of the cow is a quadrangle; below are numerous small horses.

Axial Gallery

Ibex fighting. One of them is drawn in black; the other
(with the markings on the belly) is outlined in yellow dots.
They are male Alpine ibex with long horns one above the other,
and short beards and tails. Between them is another
rectangular symbol; above them are the last of the horses
round the leaping cow.

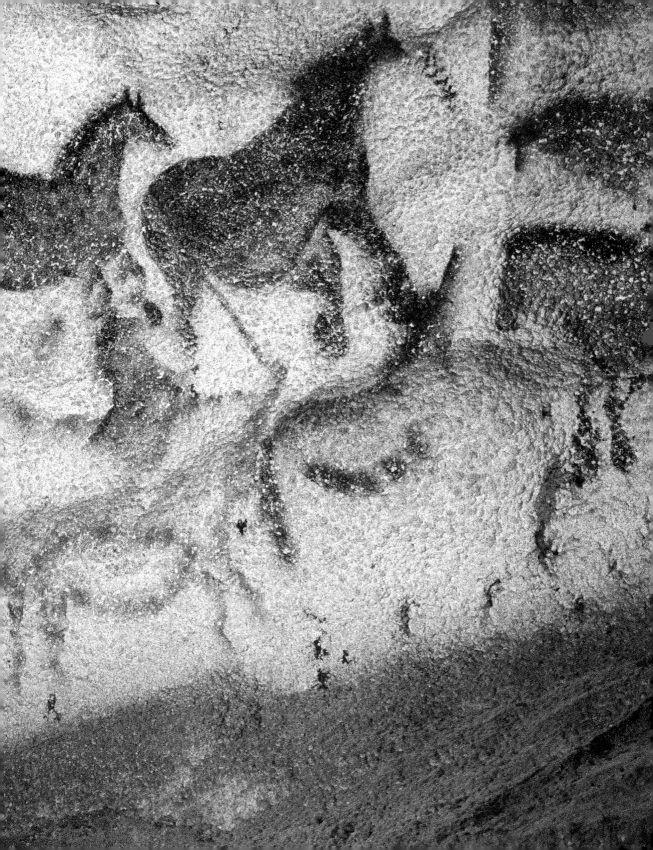

Cave mouth. By the end of September 1940, the narrow entrance passage had been widened. The roof of the cave was then clearly visible. Two openings appeared to each side of the fall of rock – the entrance to the cave itself (left) and the start of a blocked gallery (right).
Left to right: L. Laval, M. Ravidat, J. Marsal and H. Breuil. Dedication by H. Breuil to L. Laval (Delluc collection, Laval collection).

Celebrity visitors. Photographed at the end of October 1940, Count Henri Begouën, standing beside J. Marsal (left), is about to visit Lascaux with his students. They are accompanied by Father Breuil (in the light jacket) and guided by M. Ravidat (at the top of the ladder). The cave mouth has been substantially cleared (Laval collection).

Animals

Invisible yet omnipresent: Reindeer

The animal environment of Man during the Early Magdalenian Period was dominated by large herds of reindeer. Man hunted them and made use of nearly everything. Yet the animals depicted on the walls in the cave at Lascaux were of quite different species.

The reindeer predominates in this Age of the Reindeer corresponding to the Upper Palaeolithic and, more particularly, the Magdalenian Era. The animals (ranging from 1.30 to 2.20 metres in length for a weight of between 60 to 315 kg) were migratory and travelled enormous distances. Their main enemies were wolves and, in summer, the mosquitoes that pursued them from the tundra, pushing them on towards the mountains. Bucks and does had antlers with a long curved spike at the front. Their head, with a wide muzzle, was low on their chest, their withers were prominent, and they had a long dewlap below their neck. They were large animals (between 8 and 15 hands high) with tendons that cracked slightly at each step. Their feet were wide as if webbed, giving them stability on snow-covered ground. They had a short tail. They ate leaves off trees or other plants and lichen that they nosed out from under the snow. At the end of the glacial period 10,000 years ago, they left our country for the polar icecap and nowadays it is very difficult to re-acclimatise them to France.

The reindeer was a sort of prehistoric self-service. The antlers were carved into spears which were then straightened by the addition of other pierced antlers. The bones were used to make sewing needles and tubes. The hide, with its close-knit covering of hair, was tanned before being cut to make warm clothing and thick moccasins. The tendons were dissected, producing a multitude of sewing threads. The tallow was collected for use in lamps. Then there was the meat, fat, marrow and offal, all of which formed the staple meat diet of the Magdalenians, who varied their menus with berries, leaves, roots, acorns, walnuts and hazelnuts.

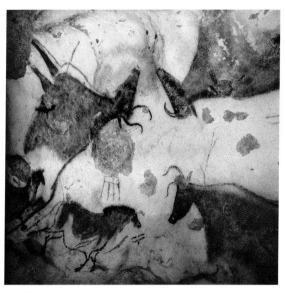

Axial Gallery. Between the Chinese horses and the Bulls' Chamber are three red cows, their heads forming a circle around a sketch of a small horse outlined in red on the roof of the gallery at its narrowest point. The body of one of the cows stretches from one wall of the cave to the other.

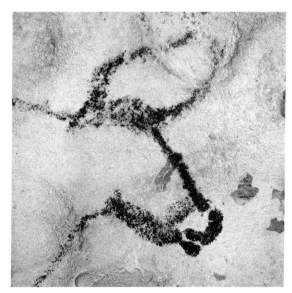

Axial Gallery. Above the leaping cow on the roof of the gallery is the head of a large black bull which closely resembles the heads in the Bulls' Chamber. Note the irregular way in which the pigment has been applied to the calcite crystals on the wall of rock.

Axial Gallery. Below the leaping cow are the famous "ponies". These five small horses are depicted trotting in a line on an imaginary stretch of ground (formed by the ledge of the rock) towards the cave entrance. The tail of one of them is shown between the raised hooves of the cow and the head of another horse. The combination of large cow and small horses is frequent in Lascaux.

A veritable bestiary

In Lascaux, the other animals seldom served as food but large numbers of them can be seen on the cave walls and roof. All of them are, of course, wild animals; none are domesticated.

Horses predominate (they are four times more numerous than cattle or deer). Most of them are small horses, very similar to Prjwalski's horses that could still be found in the 19th century in the steppes of Mongolia (they were discovered there in 1880). They lived in timorous herds led by a stallion. Nowadays, they have probably died out in the wild but large numbers of them can still be seen in zoos. They are a small breed (2.20 to 2.80 metres in length, and ranging from 12 to just over 14 hands high) with a massive head on a thick neck. The mane stands up like a brush and they have long, dark tails (90 to 110 cm in length). They have a bay coat ranging in shade from reddish to yellow-brown, and their coats are longer and lighter-coloured in the winter. The backbone is emphasised by a brown line known as a "donkey stripe" while their withers bear one or more dark markings. Their legs are also darker, sometimes with brown stripes. They do not have the same number of chromosomes as today's horses. Other wild horses are the tarpins of the steppes or forests. Common for many years in Europe and fairly similar to the previous species (with a beige or mouse-grey coat), the breed has died out over the last two hundred years. Artificially bred tar-pans were reared in the 20th century, using a cross between various tarpinoid horses including the Polish Konik. In the drawings in Lascaux (and therefore probably in the minds of the Early Magdalenians), cattle occupied second place, ranking equal with deer. Far behind the horses. The cattle in question are aurochs and bison.

The **auroch**, or primitive ox, is indicative of a more temperate climate than suggested by the presence of bison. A few figures serve to underline the strength of this animal. It was almost 3 metres in length and stood nearly

Axial Gallery. One of the "ponies". Its outline lacks detail. The mane is raised and its tail is thick and long. In the rougher parts of the painted areas are small crystals of calcite.

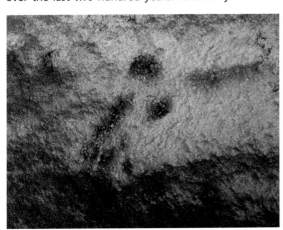

Axial Gallery. Traces and black pigment beneath the branch-shaped sign in front of the reddish horse (close-up of photo p. 34-35). A. Glory believed that the traces below once represented the head of a feline turned towards the left (round ears, forehead and muzzle).

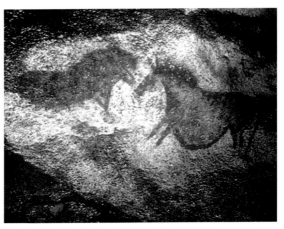

Axial Gallery. Under the black bull, two horses with bulging belly (Leroi-Gourhan collection).

Axial Gallery. The second last horse in the final turn of the passageway.Its head is drawn beneath the raised tail of the bison.

Axial Gallery. The last horse in the final turn of the passageway. Its clumsy outline follows the steeply-sloping roof of the gallery.

1.80 metres high at the withers. It could weigh anything up to one tonne. Its horns would measure 80 cm in length (cows were 25% smaller and lighter than bulls). Our domestic cattle descend from these impressive, aggressive ancestors which had a dark-brown or reddish-brown coat with a lighter stripe along the backbone. The coat was long and curly in the winter and short in the summer. The head was massive, especially in bulls which had a white ring around the muzzle and chin, a curved forehead, and long white horns with a black tip. The belly and interior of the legs were light-coloured. The aurochs lived in small herds (one bull, a few cows and the calves). The last wild ox died in Poland in 1627 but, between the wars, zoologists managed to breed neo-aurochs (which resembled the aurochs depicted on old engravings and paintings) by crossing various European breeds of cattle that were still in a very primitive stage of development. The numerous aurochs, which resembled the paintings in Lascaux, confirmed the success of this re-breeding experiment but once a species has died out, it can never be fully revived.

The other bovine present in Lascaux was the **bison**. The present European bison is its descendent and it, too, is very impressive with a length of between 3.10 to 3.50 metres, a height of 2 metres at the withers and a weight of up to one tonne. The chest is massive, and covered with long dark hair. The head hangs low and the forehead is vertical (like ours). The bison has a tuft of hair at the top of its head, and a beard. Its horns (which can reach a length of 60 cm) protrude sideways from the forehead and curve upwards then frontwards, with the tips pointing inwards. The coat is very thick but rubs off in patches during the spring when the new coat begins to grow. Bison have a short tail (50 to 60 cm) with increasingly long hair towards the tips but there is no final tuft and it looks rather ridiculous. The withers are raised because of the protuberance formed by spinal vertebrae and the cervical-dorsal line there bears four successive humps viz. the shaggy forehead, the tuft of fur between and in front of the horns, a mass of fat at the neck covered with fur and the long high withers. Once an animal of the steppes, the European bison now lives in forests. But the present bison in the Bialowiez Forest in Poland are descended from domesticated bison (hence there is a rather worrying degree of in-breeding). Left in the wild, old bulls live in isolation, forming a separate herd. During the breeding season, the herd divides into small groups (eight to ten animals), each led by the oldest cow.

A mediocre engraving in the Apse at Lascaux seems to depict a **musk ox**, or ovibus. This large goat-like creature (1.80 to 2.50 metres in length with a height at the withers of 1.10 to 1.45 metres and a weight of 200 to 300 kg) is especially remarkable for its rough, fluffed out coat that hides its shape and makes the animal look bigger than

Axial Gallery (below). The great reddish-black auroch (length over 3m) is obviously a bull. The head is shown in profile with a C-shaped muzzle emphasised by the line of the lower lip. The horns are depicted from three-quarter angle. The dewlap is protruding. The front legs are thrown forwards and one hoof is shown from front view, with the two cloots clearly visible. Covered by the body of the bull are two smaller red cows and four horned heads of young cattle. In front of the muzzle is a branch-shaped sign and an unfinished painting of a blackish-brown horse. Between the two front legs is a small hole filled with clay. It bears the imprint of scaffolding timber.

it really is. The horns, too, are very unusual. The base of each horn widens out into a plate, sometimes forming a sort of half-helmet. The horn bends downwards very close to the cheek then suddenly bends upwards like a hook. Musk oxen now live in the frozen north. In fact, they were only discovered during the 19th century. They prefer very cold climates.

The Cervides painted or engraved on the walls of the cave in Lascaux are all (with one exception, a reindeer) **stags** or **does**, which indicates a period of climatic warming. They are common deer, similar to our European Elapharus or red deer. They are 1.65 to 2.65 metres in length, 75 to 150 cm in height, and they weigh between 75 to 340 kg. The head has a pointed muzzle and is held erect. Only the buck has antlers, which are cast every winter. The long spike has numerous tines pointing forwards and it ends in a fork or palm that varies greatly from one animal to another. As the stag ages, its "head" becomes increasingly well-armed. Apart from the autumn breeding period when it calls the females by troating before mounting them, a stag lives alone or,

more often, in a mixed or all-male herd, a sort of "club" in which it spends the winter.

Ibex are now only to be found in high mountains on the edge of the snow line and are difficult to approach. When Lascaux was inhabited, they lived in our regions but did not appreciate high temperatures. These goat-like creatures, which were still fairly large (ranging in length from almost 1.15 to 1.70 metres for a height of between 65 to 105 cm and a weight of between 35 to 150 kg), had very unusual horns. They were Alpine ibex; the horns are ringed and describe the arc of a circle towards the front. They can be up to almost one metre long on males. The animals have a sturdy body and a short, sometimes recurrent, tail. They have cloven hooves, which enable them to run fast and leap across rough ground. These ibex are best-suited to the natural parks in the Alps. During the winter breeding season, males and females mix, of course. During the remainder of the year, the males live in groups while the females form a separate herd with the kids. In summer, the males clash, often participating in long, ritualised fights which decide their hierarchical position within the herd. During the breeding season, the males avoid each other. The ibex of today are well-protected from their natural predators (wolves, lynx and bears).

Axial Gallery. The falling horse (length approx. 2 m) is depicted taking a tumble. The ears turned down towards the back show fear and aggression. The hindquarters, which are represented perfectly although in a different plane, are not visible here. Around the animal are three horses and two large branch-shaped symbols.

The **felines** engraved in Lascaux, unlike the great herbivores, are relegated to a modest side passage. In fact, they are few in number (less than ten) and their outline is drawn in very summary fashion without any great detail. They are probably lions without manes (or cave lions), which differ only very slightly from the lions of today (between 1.70 to 1.90 metres in length, with the males weighing between 150 to 250 kg and females from just over 120 to 180 kg, each of them having a tuft of fur at the end of their 1 metre long tails). The mediocre drawings of them here perhaps give some indication of the cats' behaviour: prides with two or three males and five to ten females, living discreetly and, partly at least, as nocturnal animals. Lions are animals of the steppes and although nowadays their natural habitat is Africa (where they can be found even on high slopes in Kenya), they were not originally from the tropics.

The bear hiding behind a large slash of paint representing an auroch in the Bulls' Chamber is without doubt a **brown bear** (or perhaps a bear cub) and is similar to the bears of today (ranging in length from 2 to 3 metres and weighing between 150 to 780 kg, or more at the start of winter). Everybody, one might say from childhood onwards, knows its brown fur, its head with the slightly rounded forehead (unlike the forehead of its ancestor, the cave bear), its dog-like muzzle, its round ears, its front and back paws with soft rubbery pads and long curved claws that cannot be retracted, and its occasional

Axial Gallery. A black ibex and a small horse at the end of the right-hand wall of rock (close-up of photo p. 38-39).

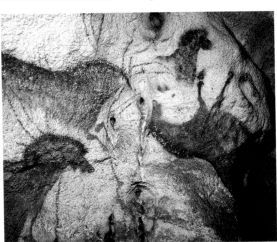

THE MEN OF LASCAUX

The artists of Lascaux were Cro-Magnons, people like us. They differed from us only in that they were taller, their skulls were less rounded and their jawlines were longer, which meant that they never had any problems with their wisdom teeth. They had the same level of intelligence as us. They lacked only the cultural education.

Digs carried out on the site of their houses show that they lived as semi-nomadic hunter-gatherers. Their tombs show their love of jewellery. They were by no means the ape-like beings dressed in rags and living in an icy wasteland full of wild beasts that have continued to be depicted in films, even in most recent times.

It all happened 17,000 years ago – almost yesterday in comparison with prehistory as a whole. Let's take a single year as a calibration device. The earliest Man, Homo habilis, appears on 1st January; Homo erectus is born in April; Neanderthal Man and early Homo sapiens take over in mid-December; and Cro-Magnon Man succeed them on Christmas Day. Lascaux is right in the middle of the "festive season".

Cro-Magnon Man. The artists of Lascaux were like us, with a few very minor differences (photos by Delluc).

propensity to stand erect. It is known that bears, which are omnivores, need a very wide territory. It is a very shy animal which hibernates in caves in winter (this is where the cubs are born and where they live for some time) and it leaves its claw marks on the clay or rock. Bears do not appear to have entered Lascaux and it would be very naïve to imagine that there was ever a battle between Magdalenians and bears or lions for possession of the cave.

Apart from all the animals which we can still see today in their natural environment or in zoos, the rhinoceros depicted in Lascaux is extinct, a fossil in fact. It is a **woolly rhinoceros** from cold climates, with cellular nostrils (this feature was inexistent or only partially developed in its predecessors). It disappeared from the planet thousands of years ago but much is known about it. Like the mammoths, numerous woolly rhinoceros have been discovered with their hide, bone and fur intact, preserved by the ice in the far north of Siberia. It was as impressive an animal as the largest of today's African rhinoceros (3

to 4 metres in length, nearly 1.5 metre tall at the withers and with a weight of up to 2 tonnes). The rather misshapen outline of the rhinoceros is familiar to everybody – a long narrow head held horizontally or bent low, large ears, bulging abdomen, short study legs, stringy tail and, of course, the two keratinous horns (the one on the forehead resembles a rose thorn while the one on the nose can be almost 1.5 metres long). The unusual characteristic of the woolly rhinoceros was its thick coat consisting of thick black underfur and long straight overhair of a reddish black colour on its flanks. The fur was particularly thick around the neck and shoulders, which increased the height of the fatty hump on its withers. It is known that Siberian rhinoceros lived alone or in a family with females and offspring, either in the steppes or in the pinewoods where it fed off the pine branches or off the lower leaves of other trees. In winter, the animals lived off their reserves of fat. Nobody knows why the species died out (like its contemporary, the mammoth, which is not depicted in Lascaux).

Axial Gallery. In the narrow turn at the end of the gallery opposite the falling horse is a red bison with an enormous hump and a raised tail, followed by two horses.

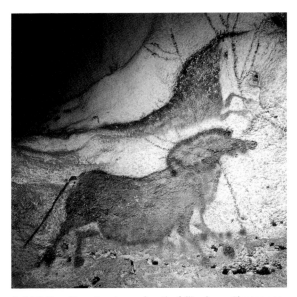

Axial Gallery. These two horses face the falling horse. The top one, with the thin head and no hind legs or belly, has raised its front legs out of the way of its companion's head. The bottom horse is complete and shows the usual graphic representation of the horse in Lascaux. Beneath its hooves is a row of dots.

Men

Setting the record straight

Lascaux does not date from the mists of time, as is shown by a few figures, albeit rounded up or down.

Life (in the form of a tiny blue algae) appeared on our planet two billion years ago. As for dinosaurs, they are 200 million years old. The first man (Homo habilis, who made the earliest-known tools) lived in Africa 2,5 million years ago. Man has inhabited Périgord for 400,000 years or a little more.

The cave at Lascaux was discovered by Cro-Magnon man 17,000 years ago. One might say, only 17,000…

People like you and me

Cro-Magnon Man resembled us physically and he had the same degree of intelligence (though he lacked our acquired cultural knowledge). Like us, he used language and was subject to tears and laughter. Like us, he had his good points and his bad. He lived an active life in a natural environment, and most of the population was young.

They were modern men and we are all Cro-Magnons. Truth to tell, our predecessor, Neanderthal Man, who lived not far away in Le Moustier for example, was already well developed. In the language of certain anthropologists, he was already sapiens (knowledgeable) As for us, we are Homo sapiens sapiens i.e. twice as knowledgeable. Or so they say.

Like us, Cro-Magnon Man, in the days when Lascaux was inhabited, was organised in a societal culture. These men were neither brutes nor tramps. They lived in comfortable huts built in the open or beneath the entrances

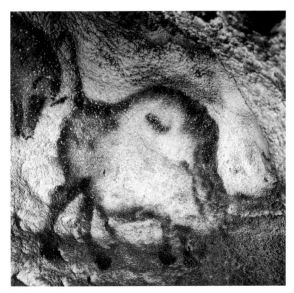

Axial Gallery. The last bison in the curve at the end. Its horns are seen from the front and it has black hooves. It has an enormous hump and its tail is held vertically.

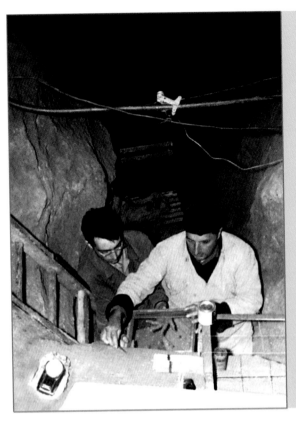

LASCAUX AND ARCHAEOLOGICAL DIGS

No digs were carried out during earthworks. Numerous documents have been lost. Father H. Breuil, S. Blanc and M. Bourgon quickly dug the base of the Pit from 2nd to 7th September 1940, searching for an offertory well or a hunter's grave. The results of their dig were spear points and a few pieces of flint. When air-conditioning was installed in 1957-1958, trenches were dug into the ground in all the galleries. Father Glory could only sketch and, in some cases, photograph a dozen valuable stratigraphic cross-sections. He picked up a few objects smothered with sand and clay, as and when he could, removing them from beneath the jack-hammers and picks. There was only one archaeological layer, containing flints, bones, pigments, etc. The only real archaeological dig was a modest affair, carried out in the base of the Pit below the scene of a man with a bison (July 1960 and July-August 1961). Father Glory discovered the famous polished pink sandstone lamp, still containing the remains of juniper. Jean-Louis Villeveygoux and Jean-Pierre Vialou witnessed the find and it was photographed by Jacques Lagrange, who was called to come as quickly as possible.

The dig in the Pit. Father André Glory undertook the only methodical archaeological dig in Lascaux in 1960-1961 (Glory collection, MNHN).

of rock shelters or caves. Gradually, they developed flint tools (blades, lamellar blades and scrapers, burins, piercers etc.) and hunting weapons made of antlers (spearheads, spear straighteners and probably spear throwers or even bows). They were not dressed in rags. The large number of needles (with eyes) found in their houses proves that they had an interest in sewing. They also had free time on their hands. A Magdalenian's day-to-day life included no more than a few hours of work, making tools, hunting, fishing etc.

These people lived the existence of semi-nomadic huntsmen, in families or groups of families. They had a base camp in the centre of the hunting territory and mobile camps near places through which reindeer had to pass (migration trails, fords, springs). They were meat-eaters, their diet being a combination of reindeer meat, fat and marrow, varied by the inclusion of wild plants. Hunting (and fishing) were doubtless reserved for the male population, as they are in all civilisations; the women were probably responsible for gathering plants. This ensured perfect environmental equilibrium.

All advanced technology (and the techniques used in the Upper Palaeolithic Era were exactly that) is accompanied by a transmission of technical information, and the method used to cut flint or antlers spread throughout Europe. In the same way, beliefs and religious rites (graves, and decorated caves) are not limited to this one area. As you know, Man is a religious animal.

Magdalenians had no villages and problems relating to population explosion were unknown. Nor did they have crops or herds. Life expectancy was short but there has been no proof of murders, war or cannibalism at that time.

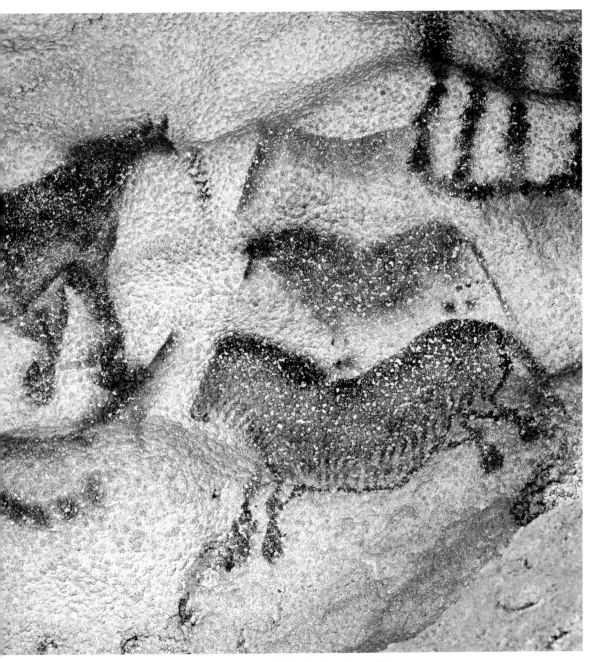

Axial Gallery. The leaping cow is surrounded by horses, some finished, others incomplete.
Some of the horses' coats are very detailed and spotted with calcite crystals.
They also have longer hair under their bellies, striped manes and shoulder markings.

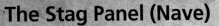

The Stag Panel (Nave)

Four old stags' heads (height of each, approx. 1 metre), drawn in black lines using manganese. Behind them is a fifth head drawn in clay. They constitute a frieze 5 metres long.

As in the Bulls' Chamber, one ear is set in the nape of the neck but, in this instance, the other ear is rather strangely placed in the side of the neck. The large antlers are drawn as elsewhere in Lascaux (one more or less vertical and the other sloping towards the back). The tear bag beneath the eye has not been forgotten. The heads are all depicted in different attitudes. It has been thought that the herd is shown crossing a ford in a stream.

Passageway. A horse engraved on a dihedron on the rock wall. Its head is turned towards the entrance to the gallery while its body is still in the Nave. One of its ears is right at the top of its head; the second lies against the neck (photo by A. and D. Vialou).

Apse. Among the mixture of engravings and paintings on the ceiling of this chamber is a superb engraving of a stag with antlers given prominence by coloured infilling (photo by A. and D. Vialou).

The Apse. The head of a stag (height approx. 40 cm.) with large antlers (one facing forwards, the other to the back). As in the stags painted in the Nave, one ear is set in the nape of the neck while the other is low down on the neck. The engraved line cuts into a rock with natural colouring and is clearly visible. All round the stag is a tangle of engraved figures that are much more difficult to decipher.

A long apprenticeship

It was Cro-Magnon man who invented the art of drawing, on the banks of the River Vézère or River Ardèche, some 35,000 years ago. It was here that several men first had the idea of tracing out, on a flat surface of the rock, a two-dimensional representation of what they saw in three dimensions in the natural environment – animals, hand prints and women's and men's genitalia. In Périgord, most of these early works from the Aurignacian are vigorous engravings on blocks of limestone or on the walls of rock shelters that have since collapsed. In Gironde, the Pair-non-Pair cave probably dates from this very early period. The Chauvet cave in Ardèche differs from the others in its ornate, carefully structured decoration.

Gradually, during the Gravettian Period (20,000 to 25,000 years ago), the number of caves decorated by these early artists increased. In Périgord, they worked mainly in small, shallow caves and the rock shelters in which they lived (Laussel, Oreille d'Enfer, Poisson rock shelters near Les Eyzies). The recently discovered cave in Cussac has some spectacular engravings of animals that make it the "cathedral" of its day, the period which also saw the decoration of Pech-Merle and Cougnac in Lot or Gargas in the Pyrenees. The outlines of the animals are still slightly gauche but the paintings of women, the famous "Venus" figures, are amazingly detailed. In the Solutrean Period (approxi-

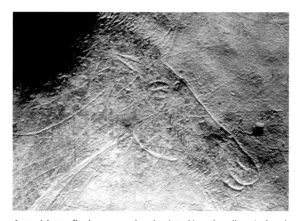

Apse. A horse finely engraved and painted in pale yellow. Its head has two eyes, set one above the other – or perhaps the artist had second thoughts. Note the many engraved lines, the stylised elongation of the head and the ears which are similar to the ones on the horse on the previous page. The erect mane and beard are characteristic of Prjwalski horses (Leroi-Gourhan collection).

Apse. The ceiling in this round chamber is covered with fine engraved lines, interlinked and intertwined, and with paintings and engravings of large animal figures, now evanescent. At the end is the entrance to the Pit (Glory collection, MNHN).

mately 18,000 years ago), great artists carved wonderful bas-reliefs of animals in a style resembling the style seen in Lascaux (Pataud-Movius and Le Fourneau du Diable in Dordogne, Roc de Sers in Charente).

The painters and engravers of Lascaux

Lascaux came into existence at the end of this long period of apprenticeship. The period between the invention of drawing (30,000 to 35,000 years ago) and Lascaux (17,000 years ago) was as long as the period separating us from the civilisation of Lascaux.

And in the light of tallow lamps, this cave appeared as the first of the deep cave-sanctuaries. The decoration of this cave is fairly stereotyped and the same layout is found throughout the Magdalenian Period, with numerous variations (as is the case in our churches). In most places, horses and cattle were represented on the main panels, surrounded by other species. The drawings of men (which are rare and very simplified) and pictures of

Felines' Gallery. At the end of the cave is a very narrow gallery that is difficult to enter. A. Glory showed the panel of cat engravings (Glory collection, MNHN).

Felines' Gallery. This painted and engraved horse is one of the small figures in this deep gallery. On the right is a sign consisting of four black dots (Glory collection, MNHN).

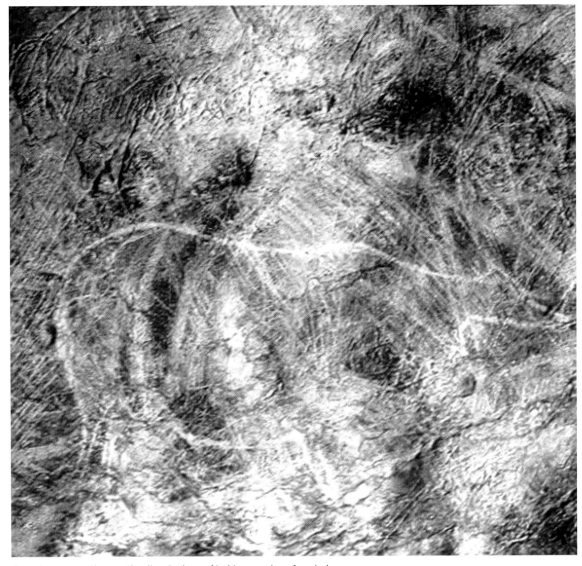

Apse. Lost among the countless lines in the roof is this engraving of a reindeer,
clearly recognisable for its low-slung head, shoulders and antlers pointing forwards.
This is the only reindeer in Lascaux yet the people of Lascaux ate almost nothing
but reindeer if the remains of their meals are to be believed (Glory collection, MNHN).

fierce animals (e.g. big cats, bears and rhinoceros) are often relegated to the ends of galleries. Geometric symbols are commonplace everywhere.

During the remainder of the Magdalenian, there were to be many other decorated caves in France and Spain, over a hundred in all, many of them very attractive but much more traditional in style (Font de Gaume, les Combarelles, Rouffignac in Dordogne, Niaux in Ariège, Altamira in Spain etc.). It was during this period that the art of making decorative objects or furnishings developed. Lascaux, like Chauvet during the Aurignacian and Cussac in the Gravettian, seems to have been a trial run and it turned out to be a masterpiece. Rather like a fireworks display beginning with the finale.

The painters and engravers were craftsmen, very probably released from the burden of their daily work by other members of the group.

They were professionals, as Professor André Leroi-Gourhan liked to say to us. Nothing is known of their living quarters but much is known about their art, their techniques and their everyday life.

It is obvious that they patiently acquired great control of their hand movements because the painted or engra-

----

The artists at work. Lascaux was one huge art studio requiring scaffolding, lighting, pigments and various tools to paint or engrave with. The artists also needed food (drawing by Michel Négrier).

MEN OR WOMEN?

In all the hunter-gatherer tribes there was a gender-based division of labour. The bloody business of hunting (and harpoon fishing) was the men's preserve and they spent several hours a day at it. The few scenes of Paleolithic hunting, such as the one in the Pit or in Villars, confirm that the hunters were men. Women spent their days looking after the children and, at the same time, processing animal products (working skins and preparing game), gathering plants and plant produce and gathering small land-based or aquatic animals. They did not take part in hunting, other than occasionally digging up or clubbing game or acting as beaters to raise game for their menfolk.

Perfect knowledge of the anatomy and ethology of the animals portrayed in Lascaux proves that the artists were also hunters. They had observed these animals over and over again in their natural environments. The obvious conclusion, therefore, is that the artists and engravers were more likely men than women.

ved lines showed a sureness that was not the result of improvisation. Drawing errors, the so-called "second thoughts", or errors in proportion are few and far between. These craftsmen had acquired real painting techniques (lightly or strongly coloured lines and flat tints). They knew how to use stencils and how to engrave, chiselling into the rock face. They invented engraving-painting-engraving. They knew how to frame the outlines of animals and make them appear to move across the rough surface of the rock face by implicitly suggesting the ground, playing with proportions and carefully positioning the animals whose outlines appear close together, adjacent, touching, cutting across each other or more or less merging into each other.

The artists remained hunters who knew every detail of the animals' anatomy, their reactions and a few more precise details. These observations of animal life were not created by the artists with a slavish will to depict reality. The outlines were reproduced with very unusual deformities (artistic devices, specific techniques and graphic guidelines) that these men had only just invented and which they systematically applied to all their drawings. Renoir did not paint women in the same way as Bernard Buffet and Giacometti's statues are very different to the ones produced by Maillol. Likewise the animals in Lascaux are not photographs of living models. The horses, aurochs, bison and stags are pot-bellied (even the males); they have sturdy legs depicted in movement and hooves painted as if seen from above (i.e. round or oval, some cloven, others not). The heads are sometimes small and elongated. The fur is suggested by a pigmented flat tint and in some cases is set out geometrically.

Perspective is carefully twisted. The head and body of the animals are shown in profile but the horns and chest of the cattle are seen from a three-quarter angle. The stags' antlers (and the horns of the ibex) are shown as being almost vertical, sloping towards the back.

Lascaux is the eye of the hunter and the hand of the artist. This is doubtless why this cave occupies such a special place in the history of prehistoric art. After Lascaux, ornamentation was very well done but in Lascaux itself, it was absolutely stunning.

WHY LASCAUX?

Father H. Breuil and Count Bégouën opted for the magic of the hunt and the depiction of game. Father A. Glory thought that shamans had taken part in ceremonies underground. This hypothesis, which cannot be proven one way or the other, was taken up again by D. Lewis-Williams and J. Clottes who added miscellaneous neuropsychological disorders such as the "three stages of trance" and drug-induced hallucinations. After A. Leroi-Gourhan, many people believed that the decoration of the "sanctuaries" reflected true religious beliefs. In fact, throughout Europe and for more than 20,000 years: 1. animal figures, limited to only a few species, were laid out topographically with the same hierarchy in the species; 2. other subjects (human beings, signs and the unspoken word) accompanied these art works; 3. the decoration of caves often seemed to be the work of real artists, professionals who worked to highlight a great idea or concept within a group. Magic, shamanism and totemism probably did exist during the Upper Paleolithic Era, but there has never been any clear proof of it.

André and Arlette Leroi-Gourhan. After Annette Laming, it was André Leroi-Gourhan studied the decorated cave walls. His wife was responsible for the study of his archaeological findings after André Glory's death (photo Delluc).

Religious art in a cave-sanctuary

The whole mythological background and heroes of the Magdalenian Period are present here viz. the fundamental dichotomy (horses and cattle), the hierarchy between other animals, Man and geometric symbols. Yet there is also much, much more.

Almost at every step, one is faced with the leitmotiv of the cave i.e. a group consisting of one large bovine and several small horses, reminding visitors that Lascaux is not just another art exhibition held somewhere in the provinces.

BLOOD, SUFFERING AND DEATH

In the bottom of the Pit in Lascaux (p. 70), there is a painting of a bison wounded by a lance or spear and losing its entrails. Yet, with its head down, it is galloping towards a prostrate figure of a man with a bird's head, his arms outstretched and his penis erect. At their feet are two objects (spear throwers?), one of them topped by a bird. This is a very exceptional scene because it tells a story whereas prehistoric art was almost never narrative in nature. It consisted only of animals, human beings and signs, without any link from one to the other, in our eyes at least – the commentary that went with them is not visible. In this scene, the wounded animal appears to be suffering as a result of its wound. Likewise in the Felines Gallery, a cat wounded by an arrow seems to be miaowing and urinating. Cave art sometimes depicts animals pierced with lines (fewer than 5 %) but usually they show no sign of being affected by their injury. Dead animals are obviously extremely rare. There is never any sign of blood flowing. Although we do not know its meanings, prehistoric art is a celebration of life.

Felines' Panel (Felines' Gallery). An engraving of a feline with a massive head, round ears, prominent shoulders and clawed feet (left) is confronting another of its species. The latter (right) has been been wounded and, like the bison in the Pit, is expressing pain. It is miaowing or vomiting and urinating (photos by Leroi-Gourhan).

Felines' Panel (Felines' Gallery). Sketch by A. Glory of the two main feline engravings. Above them is a horse, unusually shown from front view (Glory collection, MNHN).

The animals are carefully positioned to suit the appearance of the cave itself and the previous layout of the underground passages. There is a circular painted frieze in the Bulls' Chamber with the right and left halves set out in opposition to each other. There is a series of decorations in the corridor in the Axial Gallery but with a number of red cows extending up on to the ceiling, forming a sort of rose window, and a "falling" horse at the end of the gallery. The Passage and Apse have small engravings, apparently scattered at random, created one over the other so that they were probably always difficult to make out. The Nave has engravings-paintings-engravings and paintings, some in line, others not. The Pit contains drawings outlined in black (the man and bison scene) and there are engravings which are more or less intermingled in the narrow Felines Gallery.

In other words, Lascaux is a cave over 250 m long decorated with a majestic set of paintings (near the cave mouth), a miscellany of engravings (in an adjacent gallery), more engravings and/or paintings forming friezes (slightly further into the cave) and two strange smaller galleries, one of them painted, the other engraved and painted.

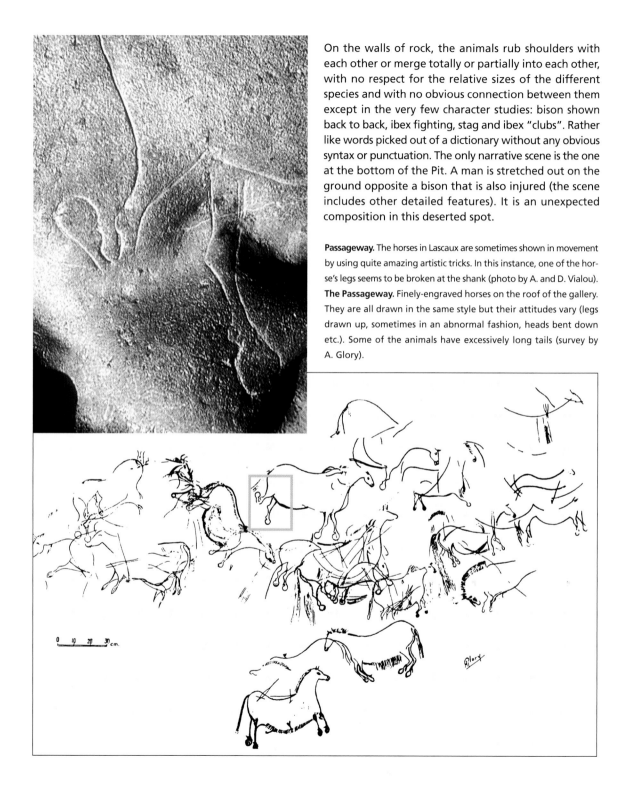

On the walls of rock, the animals rub shoulders with each other or merge totally or partially into each other, with no respect for the relative sizes of the different species and with no obvious connection between them except in the very few character studies: bison shown back to back, ibex fighting, stag and ibex "clubs". Rather like words picked out of a dictionary without any obvious syntax or punctuation. The only narrative scene is the one at the bottom of the Pit. A man is stretched out on the ground opposite a bison that is also injured (the scene includes other detailed features). It is an unexpected composition in this deserted spot.

Passageway. The horses in Lascaux are sometimes shown in movement by using quite amazing artistic tricks. In this instance, one of the horse's legs seems to be broken at the shank (photo by A. and D. Vialou). **The Passageway.** Finely-engraved horses on the roof of the gallery. They are all drawn in the same style but their attitudes vary (legs drawn up, sometimes in an abnormal fashion, heads bent down etc.). Some of the animals have excessively long tails (survey by A. Glory).

0   10   20   30 cm.

The Imprint Panel (Nave). This engraved and painted bison is more complex than it seems.
The forequarters of the first two bison, facing to the right, are slightly out of line with each other.
Cutting across the second bison head is the engraving of the hindquarters of a third animal.
Note the cloven oval hooves (Glory collection, MNHN).

The numerous, complex, and varied signs or symbols add still further to this strange atmosphere. They can be seen everywhere and can be grouped into three main categories i.e. full signs (rectangles, ovals etc.), probably representing feminine symbols, thin signs (sticks with or without lateral development) which probably have masculine overtones, and punctuation marks about which nothing is known. Some of the signs are particular to Lascaux and the few caves from the same period (rectangles in Lascaux, Gabillou and Villars) and resemble ethnic markers. Other signs, which are few in number here, are more common in Ariège or Spain (signs in the shape of a club, called "claviforms"). Yet the meaning of all these signs remains a mystery, even though there is an instinctive feeling that, in Lascaux, as A. Leroi-Gouhran said to us, Man "came very close to writing". After all, would one of our present-day signs (for example, a heart pierced by an arrow, a simple cross, or the "No Entry" road sign) be intelligible to a creature from outer space or even to one of the last "primitive peoples" of our planet?

There are other strange elements, though, in Lascaux. The animals depicted here (horses, aurochs, bison, stags, does, ibex, bears and rhinoceros) were not hunted or eaten by Magdalenian people, as shown by the scraps of bone found in the ground. Their main prey was the reindeer. And on the walls of rock, among the 600 paintings and 1,500 engravings in the cave, only one represents a reindeer. A sad thought for those who believed that cave art was a magic art form, that a guarantee of a successful hunt required no more than a few outlines of animals on a wall of rock before which the people

The Black Cow Panel (Nave). The hind legs of the black cow rest on two large partitioned rectangles (so-called "coats of arms") painted in a "patchwork" design. The outline is engraved. The panel shows a three-stage technique which is common in this gallery – an engraved sketch, a colour wash, and engraved lines emphasising the general shape and most important details. On the left is another partitioned rectangle.

Black Cow Panel (Nave). Behind the cow is a line of painted and engraved horses, moving in the opposite direction. Their legs end in oval hooves topped by a spur. On the body of the first horse is the outline of a small horse (a foal and its mother perhaps?).

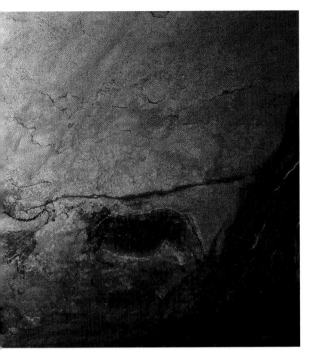

The Black Cow Panel (Nave). Two horses' heads, painted and engraved one behind the other, emerge from the rump of the black cow. Their engraved outline is partly included within the body of the cow.

The Black Cow Panel (Nave). The large reddish black cow (length 2.15 m) dominates a whole row of small horses, some of them painted and engraved, others only engraved. The pictorial representation of the cow is typical of the art work in Lascaux. A few specific details: the black-tipped horns, the short line in front of the muzzle (perhaps the cow's breath?), the protruding hindquarters, the short slender legs with narrow, elongated cloven hooves (similar to the ones on the stags) and the double line along the belly. The horses on the left have oval hooves; the ones on the right have round hooves.

could cut a few dance figures to the sound of bone pipes. It was not that simple.

And in addition to all that we can see in the cave, there is all that remained unsaid and unrepresented. In Lascaux, as in the other decorated caves, there is no attempt to depict the ground, landscape, plants, trees or rocks and there are no objects (except perhaps a sling and a spear in the scene in the Pit). Nor are there any small animals. Moreover, with two exceptions, the few animals which seem to have been wounded by spears, do not seem to be in pain.

Lascaux, a place of worship, was undoubtedly very popular. This is shown by the numerous objects left behind (more than one hundred lamps), the way in which the ground has been trodden down, and the traces of usage on the walls (rubbings, lines that are not always as expected). The artists made themselves comfortable before beginning their work. They had poles to climb up or sophisticated scaffolding (traces of this have been discovered) and the ground was covered with grasses and Artemisia in the Passage, where they had to sit down to be able to paint.

All these elements show that Art in Lascaux was designed to serve a veritable religious cult, which was organised and collective; it had no connection with any magical or shamanic rites which are always more or less marginal and short-lived, as well as being individual. People have also wrongfully spoken of witchcraft, the black magic which calls on the spirits of Evil ("it is so useful for some, expressing themselves in words that are devoid of any precise meaning, to seek precisions that the figures do not provide", said A. Leroi-Gouhran).

Lascaux is much more like a cathedral, with its nave and side aisles, than the smoke-filled lair of a magician or shaman. Yet religious motives do not preclude aesthetic objectives (or even ulterior motives relating to some

Imprint Panel (Nave). Group of horses to the left of the bison (see page 61). On the most clearly visible side are seven barbed lines and, on the horse's neck are three hooks. Yet it does not appear to be suffering from these "wounds" (Glory collection, MNHN).

Imprint Panel (Nave). A painted and engraved horse with a striped mane. Above the round hooves is a spur. The outline of the horse is engraved, using a three-stage technique used regularly in this gallery. There is an engraved sketch. Then pigment is applied and lines are used to highlight, in a paler colour, the outlines and most important details (Glory collection, MNHN).

form of magic), as we can see from the art and architecture of our Gothic cathedrals.

Lascaux, by its complexity and its graphic, symbolic and archaeological uniformity, is now considered to have been the work of a few professionals of the Faith, belonging to one or more Magdalenian families over one or more generations.

A theatre in darkness

When the cave was first discovered in 1940 and again during brutal excavations to install ventilation shafts, numerous objects were found and collected. Strangely enough, Lascaux has never been subjected to a real archaeological dig (with one exception, in the Pit, and its scope was very limited) and the ground was disturbed during the run-up to its public opening. The objects left behind by the Magdalenians form an extraordinary set of bric-a-brac, now scattered among numerous collections. Yet they have all been studied thanks to the persistence of André Glory (who unfortunately died in an accident before he could publish the results of his observations) and the determination of Arlette Leroi-Gouhran and her team (who published the main results in 1979). The complete publication of A. Glory's research is due to be published shortly, under the direction of Brigitte and Gilles Delluc. All this work has made it possible to reconstitute the life of the artists as well as of the prehistoric visitors to Lascaux.

The cave was never a home but, as people passed through it or stayed there for limited periods, numerous objects were dropped on the ground or left behind on the shelves in the rock and, more particularly, on the ground where sediment gradually covered them. The ensuing archaeological layer is quite unique, for it has none of the successive levels observed in shelters that were lived in for long periods of time. The layer is uniform and just below the surface of the ground, protected by a few inches of sand, clay or calcite. The cave itself was sealed up shortly after its use by the Early Magdalenians, when the roof in the entrance collapsed.

The objects are known to have belonged to the artists themselves, for two reasons. Firstly, the layer also contains the tools and ingredients that they used (the engravers' flints with corners rounded off by rubbing against the rock, pigments in the form of pencils or powders, pallets and crushers). Secondly, some of the objects in this layer are decorated with symbols that are specific to the art seen on the walls in Lascaux (double herringbones fitted one into the other on a sandstone lamp and a spear-head, or a star with six rays centring on a dot on a spear).

Their technical appearance shows that the flints are indeed the ones used during the Early Magdalenian Period, as are the austerely decorated spears.

The back-to-back bison (Nave). All the usual stylistic features and perspectives found elsewhere in Lascaux are present in these two bull bison with raised tails i.e. massive bodies, short legs depicted in movement, hooves seen from the front, highlighting of the background by means of strips left without pigment (legs, hindquarters). One of the bison is casting his coat as is usual in the spring. The animals can be seen acting in this way in the natural environment.

Men

The drawings in the Pit

The drawings in the Pit (total length 2.50 m) cover one wall in the deepest
corner of the cave. Two details: the artificial angle of the head
and the tail in the form of a whip. Beneath the drawings
are two barbed signs. One of them, which may be a spear thrower,
is topped by a remarkable drawing of a bird.
To the left of the man is a double series of punctuation
marks and a woolly rhinoceros.

FATHER GLORY'S RUBBINGS

Imagine yourself in the apse in Lascaux on a summer's night between 1952 and 1963. Father André Glory holds a sheet of Cellophane against the rock wall. Then, using greasepaint and working under an oblique light, he "traces" the countless intertwined lines. His assistants hold the lamp. Despite his rheumatism, the 50-year-old is perched on a scaffold. He suffers from asthma but protects himself from the hardness of the planks of wood by feather-filled eiderdowns. He is dressed in strong canvas overalls, a scarf, a beret, thick socks and heavy boots. Inside the cave, the rarified air is cold and damp (13°C with 100% humidity). The cave is full of carbon dioxide and every move makes it difficult to breathe. The problem is worsened if the smallest effort is required. The men have headaches. They are drenched in sweat. Every day, when he leaves the cave, Father Glory copies the precious lines from the tracing paper. It is hard work. From 1952 to 1963 i.e. in just over ten years, at a cost of five thousand hours of effort, he discovered more than 1,500 engraved animals and signs and created more than 100 m² of tracings.

List of engravings. From 1952 to 1963, André Glory traced thousands of engravings (Glory collection, MNHN).

And in the same layer beneath the ground, the pollens and timber residues correspond to the period of climatic warming (Lascaux' intermediate period) that is also evident in other sites, while the charcoal can be dated precisely to 17,000 B.C. by means of carbon-dating techniques.

Flashback

Let us try to imagine exactly what occurred in Lascaux. The tallow lamps project a **flickering light** on the walls of rock but it is sufficient to enable men to move around and work. The air smells slightly of burnt fat. One of the lamps looks like a thick, but highly-polished, spoon shaped out of a piece of red sandstone from what is now Corrèze (where the tiny village of Collonges-la-Rouge or Collonges the Red, is well-known). Another lamp is no more than a small block of local limestone carefully hollowed out using a flint pick. These lamps work in a closed circuit rather like old-fashioned oil lamps, with a fibre wick soaking in the melted fat.

Most of the other lamps (more than one hundred of them in all) are plain slabs of limestone no bigger than the palm of one or two hands. They are naturally flat or very slightly hollow and have not been reshaped. There are scorch marks on them (a reddened and blackened area) and experiments have shown that they worked in an open circuit like a candle. A piece of tallow was used as fuel and a small bunch of fast-burning twigs became the wick impregnated with the melted fat. This self-supporting system gives roughly as much light as a modern candle (the flame melts the tallow and produces grease which impregnates the wick). Juniper was used as a wick, as has been proven by the analysis of sooty particles removed from the lamps.

The art of **engraving** meant cutting into the coarse, sandy wall of rock with a sharp flint. The resultant line is fine, with a triangular cross-section which has now more or less worn smooth. The artists did not use complicated tools for this work; they engraved with blades, mere flakes of flint. A few of the flints (27 out of 403) still bear traces of wear on one or more corners. This would be compatible with rubbing the blade across the sandstone and limestone rock. The tools (end scrapers, burins and piercers) bear no such traces, with the exception of one burin. Some of the blades consist of small isosceles triangles; others were hafted and still bear traces of the binding agent, probably a mixture of resin and clay. Nobody knows what these blades were used for in Lascaux.

The painters extracted the **pigments** from the cave floor or from places nearby. A large quantity of coloured powders and several dozen small blocks of pigment have been found. Scratches show that these blocks were used like wax crayons, or were scraped to produce ochre powder. Iron oxides supplied the reds (haematite), in hues ranging from reddish yellow to dark reddish brown, and the yellows (goethite and clay from the cave) ranging from pale yellow to a strong brown. Manganese dioxide, black iron oxide and charcoal provided the black pigments, with shades varying from olive grey to a deep black. Crushed calcite produced a white powder. All these minerals were mixed with several parts of sand or clay, crushed in a mortar and bound with water from the cave. They were applied to the rock with fingers, with a brush made of vegetable fibre or animal hair, or with tufts of fur. The blowing of powder either straight from the mouth or through a bone pipe (a method that was often described to tourists by guides in the cave) was probably not a very common practice.

With their flickering lamps and all their equipment, the artists came face to face with the wall of rock. Most of the works of art in Lascaux are fairly high up, voluntarily spreading halfway onto the roof, out of reach. A sort of false floor was installed in the Axial Gallery, raising the ground level. We have found traces of the floor (holes into which the craftsmen slotted the beams or little ledges of rock) in the walls. In other galleries (the Bulls' Chamber, the Nave), the artists must have used roughly-lopped tree trunks, or they may have clambered up the walls of rock using the natural footholds and handholds. These various types of **scaffolding** were certainly comfortable and well-built. They were made of oak, as shown by the tiny fragments that have been examined under a microscope. Experiments have proved that it is feasible to cut scaffold poles 10 cm thick using flint tools. The remains of a length of cord were discovered near one of the small swallow-holes in the cave.

ART IN THE DAYS OF LASCAUX

In Lascaux, anatomical reality has been deformed by the artists. The animals are shown in profile, with small heads, large abdomens and short limbs in movement. The horns on the cattle are seen from a three-quarter view while the hooves are seen from above. This type of art dates back to the Early Magdalenian era: the carbon in the archaeological layer is 17,000 years old. This was confirmed by a study of pollens and the appearance of objects made of flint and hard animal material. In the same layer were pigments, flints used by the engravers and objects decorated with the same signs as those on the rock walls. Two caves in Dordogne were decorated at the same period. The narrow Gabillou cave contains engravings in the same style (but depicting numerous reindeer and several humans) and flints that can be dated to the Early Magdalenian period. The Villars cave also has the same stylistic characteristics and, more importantly, at the back of the cave has a scene that is almost identical to the one seen in the Pit in Lascaux. In both these caves, there are large grid-shaped signs reminiscent of the shields in Lascaux.

Villars Cave (Dordogne). At the end of this deep cave is an outstanding scene – a man confronting a bison, the same subject as the one depicted in the Pit in Lascaux (Glory collection, MNHN).

The drawings in the Pit. The exceptional feature of the drawing is its narrative character.
A bison is charging a man lying on the ground (a rudimentary outline of a figure with a bird's head,
hands with four fingers and an erect penis).

Nobody knows exactly how the Magdalenians were dressed but some of the objects they wore have been found. There was **jewellery** made of fossils and shells, sometimes with a slit sawn into it so that it could be worn on a thong. There is a veritable collection of prehistoric jewellery with some fifteen shells originating in the local limestone or from fossil sites in South-Western France or from the beaches of the Atlantic and Mediterranean coasts where they were collected and brought back to Lascaux, probably in stages, after being passed from tribe to tribe. This taste for jewellery was not new; it existed in the days of Neanderthal Man. Yet the unexpected feature in this case is one fake shell, a small ovoid stone engraved with scratches that imitate natural swirls. A precursor of our costume jewellery, in fact.

A prolonged stay in the cave meant that the artists had to eat, and animal bones and the remains of these meals have been found in the archaeological site of the Nave and Axial Gallery which were, in some ways, **picnic areas**. Nine times out of ten, the remains are reindeer bones; very occasionally, there are bones from roe deer, wild boar or hare. Only one or two traces of horse or red deer have been uncovered. No beef. The reindeer were young animals (between one and three years old), slaughtered early in the winter when the herd, which had spent the summer months on the slopes of the Massif Central, returned to the banks of the Vézère. This is a vital piece of information, suggesting that Lascaux was decorated in the late autumn or at the beginning of winter.

And that's it. For the moment, that's all there is to know. Modern prehistorians refuse to let their imaginations run riot. In particular, nobody knows why so many spearheads have been found throughout Lascaux. They were all broken and decorated simply, with engravings of a double interlocked herringbone pattern, a star with six rays, an elongated saltire cross, or a plain horizontal line. In these grooves (as in the swirls of one shell), there are still a few traces of red pigment, either from the powders used by the artists or perhaps from the red ochre that tanned hides or coloured the skin of the indigenous people.

The objects found in Lascaux, then, give a clear picture of the work of the painters and engravers (most of the other decorated caves do not contain any such indications). Thanks to these remains, the cave paintings can

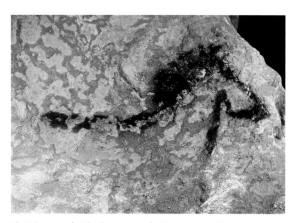

The Pit. An unfinished painting of a horse. The outline lacks precision but is similar to the ones of the painted and engraved horses in other parts of the cave. It stands opposite the scene man-bison.

be situated in time, with their graphic style and specific geometric symbols. The style is highly unusual, and was unknown to prehistorians prior to 1940, for other archaeological sites had not provided any comparable decorated artefacts. Moreover, the small number of decorated caves that were probably contemporary with Lascaux (Gabillou, Villars and the cave mouth at Saint-Cirq) were discovered later.

Four youths, scientists and modern techniques

The story of the miraculous discovery of Lascaux has been told over and over again. The marvel was revealed thanks to the obstinacy of a young man from Montignac named Marcel Ravidat, then aged 17. On 8th September 1940, with a few friends and a dog, he discovered subsidence on the hillside above Montignac. It had been caused by the uprooting of a large tree. A few days later, on Thursday 12th September, he returned to the spot with an oil lamp and a large knife, both of them homemade, in order to clear the entrance and slither down a cone of rubble. That day, he was accompanied by three other boys (Georges Agnel, Simon Coencas and Jacques Marsal). He tumbled into the cave and found his footing, quickly followed by the remainder of the group, in what we now know as the Bulls' Chamber. It was some twenty metres further on, in the Axial Gallery, that, by the smoky light of the oil lamp, the young explorers found the first paintings. They then went from one discovery to another and, on the following day, Friday 13th, Marcel Ravidat let himself down a rope into the small pothole 5 metres deep known as the Pit.

The boys' old primary teacher, Léon Laval, was told of their find a few days later. A few days after that saw the arrival of Father Henri Breuil, then considered as the "Pope" of Prehistory, followed by numerous prehistorians and a crowd of visitors. Despite the crowds, no damage was done, thanks to careful supervision on the part of the four young discoverers, and most of the easily-accessible artefacts were collected and put away in a safe place.

The earliest descriptions of Lascaux were given by F. Windels and A. Laming-Emperaire, then by Father H. Breuil. They dealt mainly with the paintings. A. Leroi-Gouhran then published a few pages describing this sanctuary-cave.

Yet it was not until nearly forty years after the initial discovery in 1940 that the meticulous graphic surveys made of the engravings by Father A. Glory were published (1,500 graphics and more than 115 metres of tracing) with a commentary by D. Vialou. Also published were the results of the scientific research carried out by a team of specialists from several different disciplines, all of us working under the leadership of Arlette Leroi-Gourhan. The research dealt with the geology of the cave, its stratigraphics, analyses of sediments (radiocarbon, wood, pollen), remains of flint and bone, lamps, shells, animals, colouring agents and access to the various walls of rock, in fact a veritable scientific analysis of the cave. Moreover, the manuscript of Father A. Glory's work in Lascaux from 1952 to 1963 was lost. It has, however, been found again and is due to be published shortly.

The paths to glory

Lascaux was a sealed cave sloping downwards and ventilated by slow-moving draughts until, in 1940, it was suddenly and brutally brought into contact with the air outside. Visits to the cave by tourists from 1948 onwards took more than one million people through it in just over fifteen years. It was thought that every precaution had been taken to ensure that the crowds would not alter or damage the works of art. A few drops of coloured water dripping from the roof of the Axial Gallery in 1955 led to the installation, using a pneumatic drill, of the ducts for a heavy-duty ventilation and airing system in 1958. Yet occasionally, the treatment is worse

than the disease and Lascaux was about to be put through the mill, as they say. It was at about this time that Mr. Ravidat noticed the first signs of the "green disease" caused by creeping plant growth that gradually spread in the warm, damp air beneath a lighting system that was almost permanently turned on.

The cave had to be closed to the public in 1963 and be decontaminated, a process that proved to be easy and did not cause any damage. It involved spraying the cave with a solution of antibiotics and formol. It was then that a new disease was diagnosed, "white disease". Calcite crystals began to proliferate because of the raised temperature, the humidity and the carbon dioxide produced by guided tours. There were few, or no, alterations visible to the naked eye but in the long run there was a high risk that calcite would completely cover the paintings.

The cave was isolated from the outside world and, after long costly research, a simple remedy was installed – the cave was cooled down by a cold spot near the entrance (this re-established the original draughts along the Bulls' Chamber/Axial Gallery, thereby concentrating condensation on this spot rather than on the walls of the cave. The naturally-produced carbon dioxide was collected and evacuated, as were any seepages of water. Maintaining the parameters at a constant level (temperature, humidity and CO_2 of the air) worked very well for thirty years. Unfortunately, in 1999, the machinery that maintained the balance of the system had to be replaced. It was a catastrophe. The pollution spread even more quickly than before and, since then, the cave has been completely closed to visitors while experts try to overcome an invasion of bacteria and mould that is much more serious than the contamination of 1963. It is hoped that their work will save the decoration in this quite outstanding cave.

The closure of Lascaux to tourists explains the success of the reproductions of the painted galleries. In 1980, the Bulls' Chamber was reconstituted by photographic techniques (life-sized colour photos were transferred onto a base made to resemble the original chamber). This exhibition can now be seen in the Musée de l'Archéologie Nationale (MAN) in Saint-Germain-en-Laye. In 1983, another reproduction was completed on the spot near the original cave – Lascaux II. In an enormous concrete bunker, there is a cement tunnel that reproduces every

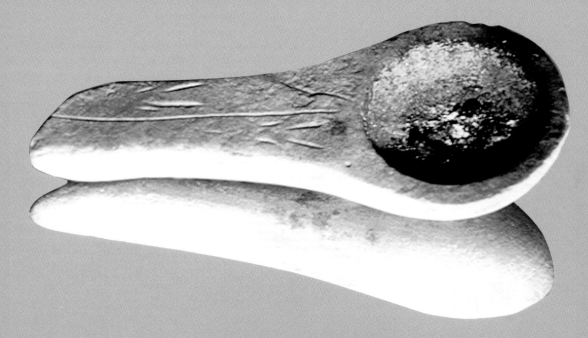

A pink sandstone lamp (length 22.4 cm). It has been carefully gouged out to form a sort of spoon shape. It worked in a closed circuit like an oil lamp. The wick has left sooty deposits and has been proved to have been made of juniper. The double interlocked chevrons engraved on the handle are similar to the ones on the walls of the cave.

Spear with a star. The spear is decorated with engraved lines reddened with ochre. Numerous spears have been uncovered in the Pit but nobody knows why they were there (photo by Delluc).

Spear with a cord. This spear tip was found in the ground of the Passageway. It still bears the marks of the cord that bound it to its wooden shaft (photo by Delluc).

Limestone bowl.
The oval bowl has been roughly shaped and still bears traces of white and red pigments. It was probably an artist's palette (photo by Delluc).

A shell and its copy. This whelk shell has a hole in it, showing it was worn as a piece of jewellery. A small pebble has been sculpted into the shape of the shell, with the start of a hole that would allow it to be worn (photo by Delluc).

Limestone lamps. More than one hundred of these rough stones used as lamps have been found. One of them (right) was shaped by striking (photos by Delluc).

Flint objects. Lascaux was not a house but it was a decorated cave that attracted many visitors. More than 400 flint objects have been found on or in the ground in Lascaux e.g. blades, tools and flints. Some of them were used for engraving (Arl. Leroi-Gourhan collection).

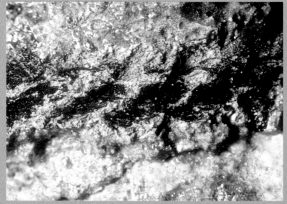

The colours of Lascaux. Numerous mineral pigments have been found, some in powder form, others as "pencils". There is manganese black, and yellow, brown and red ochres. Some of the "pencils" show signs of scraping (Arl. Leroi-Gourhan collection).

Even a rope. The imprint of a small cord with twisted strands was discovered by A. Glory in the Felines Gallery near the abyss (Glory collection, MNHN).

WORK OF HUGE PROPORTIONS

Tourism brought with it imperatives that required major work to be undertaken. This damaged the ground in Lascaux and polluted the cave.

The work carried out before the inauguration ceremony in 1948 included the widening of the cave mouth, a lowering of the level of the ground in the Passageway and Apse and the dumping of tonnes of sediment, either outside or in the Pit. Some one hundred tonnes of rubble had to be removed in 1959-1960.

In 1958-1959, all the galleries were cut into to leave space for ventilation ducts when air conditioning was installed. Father Glory could do no more than watch the enormous project take

Major work to cater for tourists. In 1948, a trench was dug at the entrance to the cave (Laval collection). In 1958-1959, the galleries suffered the same fate. Sitting beneath the first bulls, A. Glory is horrified (photo by Lagrange).

shape. The mechanical ventilation rapidly proved to be ineffective and it caused serious pollution in the cave by injecting micro-organisms into it, including algae (the "green disease"). The cave was closed in April I963 to combat the risk of crystallisation on the walls ("white disease") by decreasing the temperature, the humidity and the gaz carbonique.

After stabilisation, new work in 1999-2001 resulted in renewed proliferation of microbes and fungi. This is currently being treated.

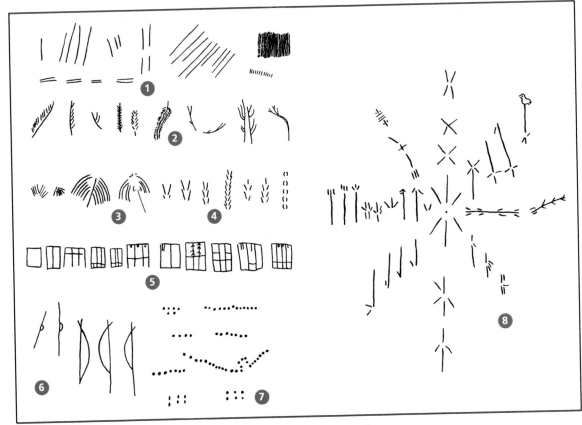

This diagram summarises the various types of sign discovered in Lascaux (400 in all).

1, single or multiple sticks drawn in parallel lines; 2, branch-shaped signs; 36, fan-shaped or "hut-shaped" signs; 4, interlocked signs; 5, quadrangles; 6, club-shaped signs; 7, punctuation marks grouped in various ways; 8, signs that are apparently derived from star-shaped signs (the star is in the centre on this drawing) (after A. Leroi-Gourhan).

detail of the walls in the Bulls' Chamber and Axial Gallery. On this background, painters have reproduced the figures and symbols as exactly as possible, using the same materials as the Magdalenians. The air-conditioned exhibition also includes a small museum illustrating the archaeological and historical environment of Lascaux, the elements used to date the finds, and the main graphic and stylistic data, all of it designed to give a closer understanding of Lascaux. A few miles away, in Le Thot, is the Centre for the Discovery of Prehistoric Art which shows visitors the stages in the construction of Lascaux II and includes a number of paintings or engravings not reproduced in Lascaux II. Among these additions is an admirable copy of the famous Pit and the three main panels in the Nave with the black cow and horses, the back-to-back bison and the Stag Frieze.

It is impossible to compare Lascaux and its reproduction. Let's just say that Lascaux II/Le Thot gives visitors more detailed information and is more accessible than anything they could have gleaned by visiting the real cave at Lascaux.

Brigitte and Gilles Delluc
Department of Prehistory
Museum national d'histoire naturelle, Paris
UMR (research unit) 5198 at the CNRS

LASCAUX 2, AN EXACT REPLICA

The project, which was launched in 1972, was completed by the Dordogne county tourism board in 1983. The new cave was housed in a concrete pillbox 200 metres from the original. The two galleries that have been reproduced here are the Bulls' Chamber and the Axial Gallery, one-quarter of the size of the actual cave but the areas containing most of the paintings. The framework consists of triple latticework strengthened by shotcrete. Together they form a self-supporting ferro-cement shell that is an exact replica of the cave. The internal skin was meticulously reproduced using data supplied by the national geographic institute (Institut géographique national). The colour and texture of the rock have also been reproduced exactly. The paintings were recreated by constantly following the model and a collection of photographic slides, using local mineral pigments (ochres, manganese dioxide). A small museum forms an antechamber to the new cave and, not far away in Le Thot, is a visitors' centre explaining prehistoric art, an ideal way of rounding off the visit.

Lascaux II. The replica recreates the largest painted galleries in Lascaux. This is the Axial Gallery seen from the end and looking towards the Bulls' Chamber (photo by Delluc).

Bibliography

AUJOULAT (N.), *Lascaux. Le geste, l'espace et le temps*, Seuil, Paris (belles photos des peintures), 2004.

BATAILLE (G.), *Lascaux ou la naissance de l'Art*, Skira, Genève, 1980, 1re éd. 1955.

BREUIL (H.), *Quatre cents siècles d'art pariétal*, Centre d'études et de documentation préhistoriques, Montignac, 1952.

BRUNET (J.), MARSAL (J.), VIDAL (P.), « Lascaux. Où en sont les problèmes de conservation? », *Archéologia*, n° 149, 1980, p. 35-50.

DELLUC (B. et G.), « Lascaux II: copie conforme », *in L'Histoire*, n° 64, 1984, pp. 76-79.

DELLUC (B. et G.) (sous la dir. de), *Le Jubilé de Lascaux. 1940-1990*, Société historique et archéologique du Périgord, Périgueux, 1990.

DELLUC (B. et G.), *Lascaux retrouvé. Les recherches de l'abbé André Glory*, Pilote 24 édition, Périgueux, 2003.

DELLUC (B. et G.), *Dictionnaire de Lascaux*, Éditions Sud Ouest, Bordeaux, 2008.

FÉLIX (Th.), BIGOTTO (Ph.), *Le Secret des bois de Lascaux*, Dolmen éditions (bande dessinée sur l'histoire de la découverte), 1992.

GLORY (A.), *Les Recherches à Lascaux (1952-1963)*, textes recueillis, présentés et commentés par B. et G. Delluc, suppl. à *Gallia Préhistoire*, CNRS, Paris, 2008.

LAVAL (F.), *Mon père, l'homme de Lascaux*, Pilote 24 édition, Périgueux (l'auteur est le fils de l'instituteur qui fut le conservateur de Lascaux pendant les dix premières années), 2006.

LEROI-GOURHAN (A.), « Grotte de Lascaux », *in L'Art des cavernes* (Atlas des grottes ornées de France), Ministère de la culture, Paris, 1984.

LEROI-GOURHAN (A.) *Préhistoire de l'art occidental*, Citadelles et Mazenod, Paris, 1995, nouvelle édition revue et augmentée par B. et G. Delluc (1re édition: 1965).

LEROI-GOURHAN (Arl.), ALLAIN (J.) et autres collaborateurs (dont B. et G. Delluc), *Lascaux inconnu*, 12e suppl. à *Gallia Préhistoire*, CNRS, Paris (le premier ouvrage scientifique consacré aux gravures et à l'archéologie), 1979.

LEROI-GOURHAN (Arl.), « Lascaux », *La Recherche*, n° 110, 1980, pp. 412-420.

LEROI-GOURHAN (Arl.), « L'archéologie de la grotte de Lascaux », *Pour la Science*, n° 58, 1982, pp. 23-33.

RUSPOLI (M.) et coll. (dont B. et G. Delluc), *Lascaux, un nouveau regard*, Bordas, Paris, 1986.

VIALOU (D.), « Lascaux et l'art magdalénien », *Dossiers Histoire et archéologie*, n° 87, 1984, pp. 61-69.

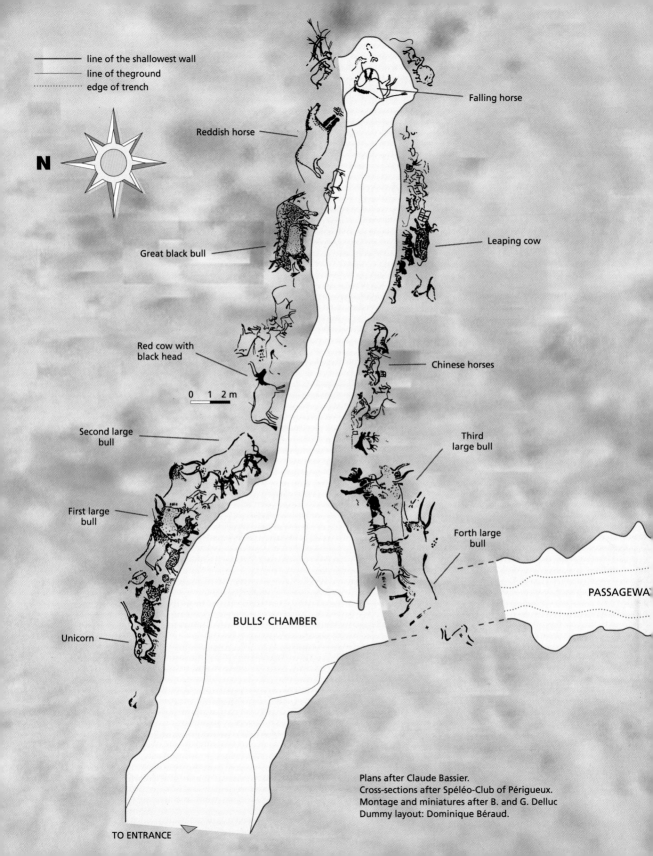

line of the shallowest wall
line of theground
edge of trench

N

Falling horse

Reddish horse

Leaping cow

Great black bull

Red cow with
black head

Chinese horses

0 1 2 m

Second large
bull

Third
large bull

First large
bull

Forth large
bull

PASSAGEWA

BULLS' CHAMBER

Unicorn

Plans after Claude Bassier.
Cross-sections after Spéléo-Club of Périgueux.
Montage and miniatures after B. and G. Delluc
Dummy layout: Dominique Béraud.

TO ENTRANCE